Corporate Acquisitions and Mergers in China

Corporate Acquisitions and Mergers in China

Maarten Roos
Rogier van Bijnen

R&P China Lawyers

This book was originally published as a chapter in Corporate Acquisitions and Mergers.

General Editor: Peter Begg

Wolters Kluwer

Published by:
Kluwer Law International B.V.
PO Box 316
2400 AH Alphen aan den Rijn
The Netherlands
E-mail: international-sales@wolterskluwer.com
Website: lrus.wolterskluwer.com

Sold and distributed in North, Central and South America by:
Wolters Kluwer Legal & Regulatory U.S.
7201 McKinney Circle
Frederick, MD 21704
United States of America
Email: customer.service@wolterskluwer.com

Sold and distributed in all other countries by:
Air Business Subscriptions
Rockwood House
Haywards Heath
West Sussex
RH16 3DH
United Kingdom
Email: international-customerservice@wolterskluwer.com

ISBN 978-94-035-2122-0

e-Book: ISBN 978-94-035-2143-5
web-PDF: ISBN 978-94-035-2180-0

This title is available on www.kluwerlawonline.com

Contents

R&P China Lawyers

R&P China Lawyers is a boutique Chinese law firm dedicated to supporting international businesses in China. Chinese lawyers and foreign consultants operate under international and foreign management and combine in-depth expertise and broad experience of the Chinese business environment with a keen understanding of the legal and practical needs of its foreign clientele.

R&P counsels mainly European and North American companies that invest in or trade with China and represents them in negotiations with Chinese counterparts and government departments. Legal services are organized around seven core practice areas: corporate/M&A; commercial transactions; compliance; employment; intellectual property; regulatory and tax; and dispute resolution.

Headquartered in China's commercial capital, Shanghai, and with a second office in Beijing, R&P's services span the country. In addition, where support is needed locally, R&P can also draw upon strong connections with government departments, law firms and leading individual specialists across Mainland China and Hong Kong.

R&P China Lawyers

17/F, Central Towers Tower

555 Langao Road

Shanghai, P.R. China

Tel: +86 21 61738270

Fax: +86 21 61738275

Email: info@rplawyers.com

Website: www.rplawyers.com

Authors

Maarten Roos founded R&P China Lawyers in 2010, and he advises international companies on M&A and other investment projects, IP rights protection and resolving commercial disputes. He also frequently represents foreign clients in negotiations with Chinese business partners and government officials and is an arbitrator on the panel of the Shanghai International Arbitration Commission (SHIAC). Maarten began his Chinese legal career in 2002, and he is fluent in Chinese.

Rogier van Bijnen is specialized in Chinese M&A and regularly advises multinationals and private equity funds on a wide range of cross-border transactions. He has lived in China since 2009 and worked as a lawyer with a Magic Circle firm in Beijing prior to joining R&P as a director in 2014.

LIST OF ABBREVIATIONS

AMR	Administration for Market Regulation
CBRC	China Banking Regulatory Commission
CEPA	Closer Economic Partnership Arrangement
CIRC	China Insurance Regulatory Commission
CIT	Corporate Income Tax
CJV	Cooperative Joint Venture
CSRC	China Securities Regulatory Commission
ECFA	Cross-Strait Economic Cooperation Framework Agreement
EJV	Equity Joint Venture
FDI	Foreign Direct Investment
FICE	Foreign-invested Commercial Enterprise
FICLS	Foreign-Invested Company Limited by Shares
FIE	Foreign-Invested Enterprise
FIHC	Foreign-Invested Holding Company
FIP	Foreign-Invested Partnership
FTZ	Free-Trade Zone
GAC	*General Administration of Customs*
GDP	*Gross Domestic Product*
MIIT	Ministry of Industry and Information Technology
MOF	Ministry of Finance
MOFCOM	Ministry of Commerce
MOFTEC	Ministry of Foreign Trade and Economic Cooperation
MOHURD	Ministry of Housing and Urban-rural Development
NDRC	National Development and Reform Commission
NPC	*National People's Congress*

PBOC	People's Bank of China
PRC	People's Republic of China
QFII	Qualified Foreign Institutional Investors
RO	Representative Office
RQFII	Renminbi Qualified Foreign Institutional Investors
SAFE	State Administration for Foreign Exchange
SAMR	State Administration for Market Regulation
SASAC	State-owned Assets Supervision and Administration Commission
SAT	State Administration of Taxation
Shanghai FTZ	China (Shanghai) Pilot Free-Trade Zone
SHIAC	Shanghai International Economic Trade Arbitration Commission
SOE	State-Owned Enterprise
SPV	Special Purpose Vehicle
VAT	Value Added Tax
VIE	Variable Interest Entity
WFOE	Wholly Foreign-Owned Enterprise
WTO	World Trade Organization

1 INTRODUCTION

1.1 The Increasing Importance of China

[01] China's modern economic history started in 1978, with the decision to open China to the outside world. This decision led the country onto a path of phenomenal economic growth and development. Measured by GDP, China is now the second-biggest economy. In recent years, the growth rate has slowed down as the economic focus has shifted from production to consumption and services. Despite recent setbacks such as the trade war with the United States, China continues to grow at a much faster rate than the developed world. Having cemented its position as a key player in the global economy, the only question remains how dominant it will become economically in the years to come.

1.2 Foreign Investment in China

[02] A big part of China's success story has been the government's willingness to allow foreign investment into China. It is well known that companies from all over the world have flocked to China to build manufacturing operations, to engage in trade and to sell services. This trend was initially started by large multinationals, but hordes of small- to medium-sized businesses have gradually followed. While success has not been a guarantee, many of these firms have benefited from the opportunities that China offers.

[03] What is not always realized, however, is that China's economic development did not only attract a lot of foreign investment, but foreign investment has in fact been one of the major engines of China's economic miracle. The government has used economic policy to attract and guide foreign investment into the sectors it deemed important for its continued development. Starting in the late 1980s, for example, foreign investors mostly focused on manufacturing industries, producing mainly for export markets, because China's laws and policies were structured to provide manufacturers with the best possible environment to enter China, set up their factories, manufacture their goods and export these to foreign markets. A stable economic environment and good infrastructure, access to inexpensive labour and other key resources, and tax benefits were some of the tools that China successfully used to attract huge amounts of funds and expertise, which were used to bring the economy to a higher level.

[04] China's accession to the World Trade Organization (WTO) in 2001 heralded a change in industrial policy. While all manufacturers continued to receive favourable treatment, new industries were opened for foreign investment as well. Foreign investors were invited to invest in manufacturing sectors that were previously regarded as too sensitive to be allowed outside influence. But even more crucial was the decision to open many service sectors to foreign companies and allow foreign-invested companies to engage directly in international trade and domestic distribution. In 2008, China's tax laws stopped favouring foreign investment, but China's top-notch infrastructure, the improving legal and administrative environments and the gradual build-up of its domestic market more than made up for this.

[05] In recent years, some observers have seen China's development lose some of its shine. Indeed, it is becoming increasingly difficult for China to continue the ferocious pace of development that it has kept up for so long, especially as domestic consumption and services are relied upon to bring the economy to the next level. Problems such as income disparities, pollution, higher costs and corruption are becoming more obviously intrusive in a country of which many parts can now be regarded as distinctly middle-income.

[06] Moreover, China's position in the world is also changing. The Western world is increasingly concerned about China's development, focusing on China's economic policies, the way it treats foreign businesses and the perceived slow pace of market opening. The trade war that the United States started in July 2018 with tariffs on Chinese goods for alleged unfair trade practices continues to date. Pressure from the United States and Europe could result in improvements to China's legal environment, but there is also risk of a backlash against foreign companies operating in China.

[07] In any case, the country's leaders are actively taking steps to respond and deal with these challenges, while at the same time keeping a tight rein on politics. Pessimists have been predicting the demise of the Chinese economic miracle for decades, but so far China remains a very promising place for foreign companies to take their business.

1.3 Trends in M&A

[08] While most foreign investors continue to invest in China through traditional greenfield investment structures, the use of mergers and acquisitions (M&A) has in recent years become an increasingly popular means to expand into China, not only with large multinationals but also with mid-sized transnational companies and even small- to medium-sized foreign businesses. Several developments have contributed to this trend.

[09] First, China's fast-pace development is creating an increasingly competitive economic environment, in which M&A presents a valuable channel to gain a head start. Many foreign investors no longer have the time and patience to gradually build their operations in China but instead opt for gaining market access, enlarging the customer base and/or taking on production capacity immediately.

[10] Second, many foreign investors choose an acquisition to take advantage of opportunities resulting from domestic trends. Some years ago, for instance, the privatization of State-Owned Enterprises (SOEs) and the sell-off of state-owned assets increased the number of potential acquisition targets available to foreign investors. At present, consolidations may be driven in part by efforts of industry players to restructure and modernize the industrial landscape at the encouragement of the government, creating new opportunities for foreign investors that have sufficient capital and technical know-how to purchase a valuable position in the market. The increasing importance of enhancing productivity through technical applications, as opposed to the simple accumulation of resources, plays an important role as well – especially considering the ever-increasing costs of labour and other resources.

[11] A third explanation for increased inbound M&A activity is the gradual shift in focus of foreign investors from manufacturing for their home markets to serving the China market. Parts of China have already progressed from low-income to middle-income, especially in first- and second-tier cities in the eastern parts of the country. Recognizing this progress, metropolitan areas, such as the Yangtze River Delta (around Shanghai), the Pearl River Delta (in southern China) and the area around Beijing, form attractive markets for a wide array of products and services. Establishing distribution networks, however, is expensive and time-consuming, while manufacturing for and marketing to Chinese businesses and consumers require knowledge of local preferences and customs. Acquiring an existing company can be a valuable stepping stone to procuring the knowledge and contacts necessary to expand quickly into the Chinese market.

[12] *Finally*, there is no doubt that acquisitions by foreign investors have also become increasingly practical. Regulators have done much to improve the regulatory framework for cross-border M&A activity, and acquisitions have become much more straightforward to initiate and implement. Meanwhile, improvements in corporate governance are leading to greater transparency in local companies and a better understanding of Chinese business culture and the adoption of international management practices have made the integration of a domestic company into a global group less daunting. Although there are still plenty of hurdles, the combination of these developments has expanded the opportunity for investors to reap the full benefits of a merger or acquisition.

[13] At the same time, some characteristic challenges remain. Besides legal restrictions and approval procedures that remain more complicated than in many other jurisdictions, dealing with Chinese target companies often requires a lot of attention. Many Chinese businesses are organized in ways that are difficult for potential foreign buyers to comprehend, and decision-making within such companies is often far from transparent. Many private companies have grown up in a legal environment that was (and to a certain extent, still is) not fully developed, which can create risks that – at least on paper – are difficult to accept by foreign companies that are used to doing business in a more mature legal environment. In other words, suitable acquisition targets can be difficult to find, and for the good ones, there may be more than one suitor. China's continued attractiveness as a growth market gives the most bargaining power to sellers that are operating in accordance with international standards.

1.4 Structure of This Publication

[14] In Chapter 2 'Restrictions on Foreign Investment', we will discuss which restrictions foreign investors face when investing in China. This includes special regulations that apply to particular industries in which foreign investment remains prohibited or restricted, the need for special legal entities in other cases, licensing requirements for certain industries, requirements for approval or record-filing for foreign investments, additional restrictions for listed companies and foreign exchange controls. We will also discuss how restrictions have been gradually lifted by testing new policies first in free-trade zones, after which these are rolled out nationwide, and how the new *Foreign Investment Law*, adopted in March 2019 and to take effect on 1 January 2020, is providing for further liberalization, equality and protection. Finally, we set out some of the restrictions Chinese investors face when making outbound investments.

[15] Chapter 3 'Business Vehicles' is about the legal entities available to foreign investors in China. For now, when a foreign investor invests in a new or existing Chinese legal entity, the entity gets a special name and status: Foreign-Invested Enterprise (FIE). However, when the *Foreign Investment Law* takes effect in 2020, foreign investors will have to incorporate regular PRC business vehicles that are subject to the provisions of the *Company Law*. Furthermore, the general rules of the *Company Law* also apply to FIEs, unless specific FIE legislation states otherwise. We will, therefore, start Chapter 3 'Business Vehicles' by providing a basic overview of the PRC corporate legal framework under the *Company Law*. Thereafter, we will discuss each of the different kinds of FIEs available to foreign investors and the relevant establishment procedures and restrictions on capitalizing and financing FIEs. We will also discuss a few corporate forms available to foreign investors that are generally not considered FIEs.

[16] In Chapter 4 'Mergers & Acquisitions', various types of private M&A by a foreign investor will be discussed: the acquisition of an entire domestic-owned company, the partial acquisition of a domestic-owned company, the acquisition of an FIE, an investment by an FIE in a domestic-owned company, an offshore transaction, a subscription for newly issued equity, a share swap, an asset acquisition, a merger and the acquisition of state-owned assets. Each of these transactions is subject to different rules and regulations, and all require either government approval or a record-filing in the PRC. Note that public M&A falls outside the scope of this publication (although we will briefly touch upon this in the context of Chapter 2 'Restrictions on Foreign Investment').

[17] This publication reflects the state of the law until *31 October 2019*.

1.5 Abbreviations and Short-Form References

[18] In this publication, we refer to various government ministries and departments and certain legal concepts. At first mention, we will provide the full name as well as its common abbreviation (e.g., Ministry of Commerce/MOFCOM, *Foreign-Invested Enterprise*/FIE), while in the remainder of the text we will refer to the abbreviation only. We provide a full list of all abbreviations used throughout herein at the beginning of the publication.

[19] Foreign direct investment in China is regulated by numerous laws, ministerial regulations and rules at the local level. In this publication alone, we refer to about a hundred and fifty pieces of legislation. Since the full names of Chinese rules and regulations tend to be unusually long, we have used a system of unofficial short-form names for each piece of legislation. At the end of this publication, we have included a table that lists their full names (both in English and Chinese), with relevant details (e.g., effective date and issuing authority).

[20] The short-form references to laws, rules and regulations are all stated in *italic font.* References to laws include the word *law* at the end (e.g., the *Company Law*), and references to rules and regulations are in most cases preceded by the year in which they were first promulgated (e.g., the *1983 EJV Implementing Rules*).

2 RESTRICTIONS ON FOREIGN INVESTMENT

2.1 Industries Restricted for Foreign Investors

2.1.1 The Foreign Investment Negative List

[21] In the past, the *Foreign Investment Catalogue* (and the *Central and Western China Catalogue* focusing on foreign investment in relatively underdeveloped areas in Central and Western China) was always the starting point for any research regarding restrictions on foreign investment in China. This catalogue, jointly issued by the Ministry of Commerce ("MOFCOM and the National Development and Reform Commission (NDRC), sets limitations to foreign investment in China. The catalogue was first introduced in 1995, and the last edition was completed in 2017. The catalogue contained a detailed list of specific industries divided into three categories: '"encouraged", "restricted" and "prohibited"'. Any industry that was not listed in the catalogue would automatically fall within the fourth category: 'permitted'.

[22] Over recent years, however, China has gradually implemented a system of negative lists – listing only those sectors that are '"restricted" or "prohibited"' to foreign investment. The first negative list was issued in 2014 for the Pilot Free-Trade Zone in Shanghai (*see* below), while the first nationwide negative list (applying nationwide but not in pilot free-trade zones) was issued in 2018 and later updated as the *2019 Foreign Investment Negative List*. The *Foreign Investment Catalogue* continued to exist until July 2019 when the last part of this catalogue – the determination of which sectors should be encouraged to foreign investment – became obsolete with the adoption of the *2019 Catalogue of Industries for Encouraged Foreign Investment.*

[23] Over the years, every update of the catalogue/negative list has led to a slow but steady easing of restrictions on foreign investment. The *2019 Foreign Investment Negative List* is no exception: compared to the 2018 version, the number of sectors subject to restrictions was reduced from forty-eight to forty, and restrictions were eased in several sectors within the service, agricultural and manufacturing industries. To give some examples, in the value-added telecommunication service sector, the restrictions on foreign investment in domestic multiparty communication, store-and-forward business as well as call centres have been cancelled, and in the agricultural sector, foreign investment in the development of wild animal and plant resources is no longer prohibited.

[24] However, various sectors remain entirely prohibited to foreign investment (e.g., internet news services and online publishing services; news agencies; compulsory education institutions; and Chinese legal services), and in other cases, foreign investment is permitted but subject to restrictions, for example because the Chinese party must be the controlling shareholder (e.g., investment in the printing of publications; nuclear power plants; domestic water transportation).

[25] It has been mentioned that the first negative list was issued for the *China (Shanghai) Pilot Free-Trade Zone*, in 2014. In fact, several negative lists exist that do not apply nationwide but are still important. Part of the reason for the establishment of the first pilot free-trade zone in 2014 was to allow it to experiment with foreign investment for which the rest of China was not yet deemed ready. Since then, pilot free-trade zones were established across the country and several of these have adopted their own negative lists. The *2018 FTZ Negative List* was the first negative list that covers all the free-trade zones and so may be seen as an attempt to create a level playing field – though local rules and variances continue to exist. Besides local significance, the negative lists of the pilot free-trade zones have considerable value in predicting which sectors may open to foreign investment nationwide in the near future.

[26] The latest version the *2019 FTZ Negative List* contains 37 items and contains many of the same prohibitions as the *2019 Foreign Investment Negative List*. However, a few of the sectors prohibited or restricted for the rest of China are not listed in the *2019 FTZ Negative List* at all and are therefore permitted (e.g., fishing aquatic products in sea areas under Chinese jurisdiction and in inland waters; printing of publications); while for others, the restrictions are less severe. As such, the *2019 FTZ Negative List* continues to be a model for future liberalizations though with restrictions focusing on sensitive sectors, the process of further opening up may be slowing down.

[27] While the negative lists focus only on restrictions, the *2019 List of Industries for Encouraged Foreign Investment* now has the sole function to detail in which industrial sector's foreign investment is encouraged. Continuing previous policies, it also includes a separate section to stimulate foreign investment in certain specific areas in Central and Western China. Benefits available to the industries in this 2019 Encouraged List vary but may include tariff duty exemptions for imports of self-use equipment, preferential rates for corporate income tax and discounted prices for investment in land.

[28] Compared to the 2017 versions, the *2019 Catalogue for Encouraged Foreign Investment* expands the range of *encouraged* industries for foreign investment from 987 to 1108 sectors (*incl.* 415 items encouraged nationwide, and 693 items encouraged in Central and Western China). The main focus is on industries that China is trying to promote such as modern agriculture, advanced manufacturing, high technology, energy conservation and environmental protection as well as modern services. Some of the items that have been added in 2019 include: the electronic information sector (e.g., 5G core components, IC etching machines and cloud computing devices); the equipment manufacturing sector (e.g., industrial robots, new-energy cars and key components for smart cars); the modern pharmaceutical sector (e.g., key raw materials for cell therapy medicine and large-scale cell culture products); the new material industry (e.g., new materials for aerospace, monocrystalline silicon and large wafers); and in the service industry, the business service sector (e.g., engineering consultancy, tax and accounting), the commercial circulation sector (e.g., cold chain logistics, e-commerce) and the technology service sector (e.g., artificial intelligence, cleaner production, carbon capture and circular economy).

2.1.2 The Domestic Catalogue

[29] In addition to the *2019 Foreign Investment Negative List,* which only applies to foreign investors, the State Council has also issued the *Domestic Catalogue* (last amended in 2016), which applies to both domestic and foreign investors. This catalogue contains twelve categories of industries, and for each category, detailed investment projects have been described that require government approval. Given the sensitive nature of the projects in the *Domestic Catalogue*, such government approval may be difficult to obtain in practice.

[30] Most of the projects in the *Domestic Catalogue* relate to large-scale infrastructure projects, such as water reservoirs, power stations, coal mining, oil refining, rail and highways, telecom networks, petrochemicals, aerospace, and urban roads, bridges and tunnels. Other categories include automobile and tobacco manufacturing and large-scale theme parks and national tourism sites.

2.1.3 Preferential Treatment for Hong Kong, Macao and Taiwan Investors

[31] Investments in Mainland China made by an investor incorporated in Hong Kong or Macau may receive preferential treatment under the Closer Economic Partnership Arrangement (CEPA) (first signed in 2003, last supplemented in January 2019),[1] while Taiwan investors may benefit from the Cross-Strait Economic Cooperation Framework Agreement (ECFA) (signed in 2010). These arrangements

[1] In November 2015, an additional *Agreement on Trade in Services* was concluded, which made certain benefits available in the whole of China that were previously only available in Guangdong Province; *see* the *2016 Mainland Measures*.

provide companies from Hong Kong, Macau and Taiwan preferential access to several sectors, including real estate, construction, education, recruitment, medical, telecommunications, banking, securities and accountancy.

[32] The benefits, which vary per sector, include early market access (i.e., access to certain industries still closed for other foreign investors), lower entry requirements (e.g., lower registered capital requirements) and larger equity holdings (i.e., a larger equity percentage may be held in some restricted industries compared to other foreign investors).

[33] *CEPA* imposes several qualification criteria in order to prevent foreign investors from outside Hong Kong and Macau from simply setting up a special purpose vehicle in one of these jurisdictions to enjoy the special benefits. The most important requirements are that the Hong Kong or Macau company needs to be established for at least three years, have substantial operations in Hong Kong or Macau, and pay profit tax in Hong Kong or Macau.[2]

[34] However, no limitation is set on the ownership of the Hong Kong or Macau company. Therefore, an investor from, for example, Europe could consider acquiring a company in Hong Kong or Macau that meets all these criteria, and then use this company as a vehicle to further invest in Mainland China.[3]

2.1.4 Circumventing Restrictions: Variable Interest Entities (VIEs)

[35] Given the appeal of China's economy and its businesses, Chinese companies and foreign investors do sometimes work together to circumvent some of the above restrictions, thereby enabling foreign investors to invest in Chinese industries that would otherwise be closed to them. The most popular method is the so-called Variable Interest Entity (VIE). Under a VIE structure, a Chinese-owned company (the VIE) holds all licences and carries out all activities prohibited or restricted for foreigners, while the foreign investor takes on the risk and benefit of the entrepreneurial activity.

[36] In practice, the foreign investor's vehicle – in some cases a foreign company but more often an Foreign-Invested Enterprise (*see* section 2.2 'Foreign-Invested Enterprises' below) – usually obtains a set of contractual rights vis-à-vis the VIE (e.g., pledges, voting arrangements, licensing agreements). These contractual rights allow the foreign investor's vehicle to exercise control over the VIE (so consolidation of the financial accounts is possible), with all economic benefits transferred back to it (allowing the foreign investors to enjoy the profits of the restricted business). As an example, many large Chinese companies operating in *prohibited* or *restricted* industries have used a VIE structure to get listed on an overseas stock exchange (e.g., Alibaba and Baidu).

[2] An enterprise incurring losses can still qualify if it has substantial business operations in Hong Kong or Macau.

[3] Similar rules apply for Taiwan under *ECFA*, but Taiwan has been a far less popular route.

[37] This structure is, however, not without risk. Besides the common challenge of practical control, it is unclear whether the contractual arrangements between a VIE and the foreign investor's vehicle are enforceable in the PRC given that they are clearly designed to circumvent the law. In fact, the first draft of the *Foreign Investment Law* (published for comments in 2015) specifically prohibited the circumvention of foreign investment restrictions through a VIE structure (*see* section 2.1.4 'Circumventing Restrictions: Variable Interest Entities (VIEs)' above). That these provisions were removed in the final version of the law may be a sign that China is not yet ready to tackle the structure – though this situation may not last forever.

2.2 Foreign-Invested Enterprises

[38] When a foreign investor establishes or acquires equity in a Chinese company, such company becomes what is generally referred to as an Foreign-Invested Enterprise (FIE) – a special designation for a Chinese company that is owned wholly or partially by one or more foreign investors. The various legal entities available to foreign investors will be extensively discussed in Chapter 3 'Business Vehicles', and at this point, a brief summary of these legal entities is sufficient.

[39] It should be noted that when the *Foreign Investment Law* becomes effective on 1 January 2020, companies that are newly established with foreign investment or domestic companies that are acquired (whole or in part) by foreign investors will no longer be subject to the rules that now apply to FIEs. Instead, these companies will be subject only to the *Company Law* and be treated the same as companies with Chinese investment only, particularly in respect of organizational form, corporate governance and standard of conduct. However, existing FIEs will be permitted to continue their current corporate form during a five-year transition period, and so in the near future little will change for these existing FIEs. Moreover, there is little information available on how these FIEs will be turned into 'ordinary' legal entities, and so it seems early to start anticipating this development. As such and at least for now, understanding the types of FIEs that are available to foreign investors remains an important part of understanding China's legal landscape.

[40] The Foreign-Invested Enterprises available for foreign investment in China include:

(a) Wholly Foreign-Owned Enterprise (WFOE)
(b) Equity Joint Venture (EJV)
(c) Cooperative Joint Venture (CJV) and
(d) Foreign-Invested Company Limited by Shares (FICLS).

[41] In common terminology, several other abbreviations are used as well. The most common examples are the Foreign-Invested Holding Company (FIHC) and the Foreign-Invested Commercial Enterprise (FICE). In each of these cases, the name is not to indicate another type of FIE; instead, it is about the function of the company (e.g., an FIHC is a company whose predominant function is to invest in

other domestic entities, while an FICE is a company engaged in trading and distribution). As such, an FIHC could be a WFOE, EJV or FICLS.

[42] The FIE is subject to requirements or restrictions that do not apply to 'ordinary' domestic legal entities. As a result, foreign investors have less freedom compared to domestic investors when structuring their investments in China. The most important restrictions include approval requirements or a record-filing for incorporation, rules on thin capitalization and less freedom to select a tailor-made corporate governance system.

[43] As background, when China permitted foreign investment for the first time in 1979 through joint ventures, a general law for all companies had yet to be adopted. The Chinese government, therefore, had to create special legislation in order to enable foreign investment (first the *EJV Law* and later also the *WFOE Law* and *CJV Law*). This practice of having distinct entities for foreigners became so embedded in the Chinese legal system that it was never completely abolished, even after the introduction of the *Company Law* in 1993 and subsequent amendments. However, as mentioned, this is going to change with the *Foreign Investment Law* taking effect on 1 January 2020.

[44] Three other vehicles available to foreign investors (but not considered an FIE). are:

(1) Representative Office (RO) – not considered an FIE since an RO is not a Chinese legal person
(2) Foreign-Invested Partnership (FIP) – not considered an FIE since an FIP is not an enterprise, but a partnership and
(3) *Domestic subsidiary of an FIE* – not considered an FIE, since it is a regular Chinese company without any direct foreign shareholding.

2.3 Industry-Specific Restrictions

[45] There are over a hundred business activities in China that require additional, industry-specific licences. These restrictions, which apply to both domestic and foreign investors, are currently scattered over numerous regulations and rules issued by various industry regulators. Prior to making any investment, a foreign investor should, therefore, not only check the *Foreign Investment Negative List* to confirm whether the investment is permitted but also whether its particular business activity or industry is subject to any specific regulations.

[46] In order to make it easier for businesses to identify whether their activities require a licence, in March 2016, NDRC and MOFCOM published the *Draft Market Access Negative List* (pilot version), setting out which business activities are prohibited in China and which activities are subject to licensing. The *Draft Market Access Negative List* was effective in the Free Trade Zones (*see* section 2.7 'Pilot Free Trade Zones') on a pilot basis, while the official *Market Access Negative List* has been rolled

out nationwide in 2018. Note that the *Market Access Negative List* applies to both domestic and foreign investors and is different from the *Foreign Investment Negative List* discussed above (section 2.1.1 'The Foreign Investment Negative List') that only applies to foreign investors.

[47] Even though domestic investors are generally subject to similar restrictions, for some regulated business activities, different rules and regulations still apply if these are carried out by an FIE. The criteria to qualify for relevant licences can, therefore, be more burdensome, or at least different, for foreign investors compared to the rules that apply to their domestic peers.

[48] Industry regulations may set a minimum amount of registered capital that a foreign investor needs to contribute to its legal entity in China; although, the *2015 FIE Registered Capital Decision* removed this requirement for many industries. Another common requirement is a minimum of net assets that the foreign investor itself needs to have on its books. Foreign investors may also need to prove a certain track record, such as a minimum number of years of operating history in the relevant industry and experience criteria for key personnel it intends to dispatch to China. Soft criteria may include a clean history (e.g., no past convictions or violations of laws) and the requirement to have all necessary operating systems in place.

[49] Criteria with respect to the foreign investor itself (e.g., assets or experience) are known to be problematic when the foreign investor prefers a China set-up via a new special purpose vehicle (e.g., in Hong Kong), since this SPV will have no assets and operating history. It is then at the discretion of the local regulator to determine whether it will accept any evidence that this SPV's ultimate parent satisfies the relevant criteria. We have seen examples of industry regulators interpreting the relevant rules with flexibility, while others simply reject the application.

[50] All qualification criteria regarding the foreign parent obviously apply when an FIE obtains its initial licence for the relevant business activity, but they also need to be complied with when a foreign buyer acquires a domestic target. In such case, the buyer needs to demonstrate that it meets all relevant qualification criteria for the foreign parent, otherwise the transaction will not be approved.[4]

[51] Examples of activities for which specific requirements apply in case of foreign investment include *construction* (skill qualification required and certain work experience criteria apply for foreign managers),[5] *medical treatment* (the Chinese side to hold at least 30%, minimum CNY20m total investment and certain experience criteria),[6] and *telecom* (minimum registered capital requirements, foreign ownership restrictions, and criteria regarding experience and operating history).[7]

---

[4] Article 4 *2006 M&A Rules*; Art. 4 *1997 FIE Acquisition Rules*.

[5] *2002 FIE Construction Measures*; *2003 FIE Construction Implementing Rules*.

[6] *2000 FIE Medical Institutions Interim Measures*; there are however opening-up initiatives, *see* the *2013 Shanghai FTZ WFOE Medical Institutions Tentative Measures* for the Shanghai Free Trade Zone and the *2014 WFOE Hospitals Notice* on a pilot in seven (city) provinces; CEPA also relaxed certain criteria for Hong Kong and Macau investors.

[7] *2008 FIE Telecom Enterprises Provisions (revised in 2016)*.

[52] Like in many jurisdictions, financial services are heavily regulated in China. Foreign investors may be subject to additional scrutiny as well. For example, foreign investors in domestic insurance companies need to meet more onerous qualification requirements in terms of profit track record, total assets and credit rating compared to their domestic competitors.[8] A foreign investor in a foreign-invested securities company is also subject to more onerous qualification requirements and, in some cases, first needs to qualify under a special regime (such as the CEPA with Hong Kong) before it is permitted to invest. However, even in financial services, China is making steps to relax control; in a recent circular, the State Council cancelled restrictions on the business scopes of financial institutions, such as foreign banks, securities companies and fund management companies.[9]

2.4 Investment Approvals

[53] All foreign investment in China (both greenfield and M&A) requires either a government approval or a record-filing. In contrast, PRC investors often do not require such investment approval or record-filing, and even when they do, they usually face less scrutiny. However, we have seen much improvement in the past few years. In section 2.4.2 'MOFCOM Approval or Record-Filing', we will discuss the recent cancellation of MOFCOM approval for industries outside the *Foreign Investment Negative List*, while in section 2.7 'Pilot Free Trade Zones', we set out the exceptions that already apply in the *Shanghai Free Trade Zone* and some other free trade zones, while further liberalization is expected after the *Foreign Investment Law* takes effect in January 2020 (section 2.8 'The Foreign Investment Law').

[54] The key PRC regulators approving foreign investment are MOFCOM and NDRC. In addition, the State Administration for Market Regulation (SAMR) (previously known as the *State Administration for Industry and Commerce*) is responsible for company registration and issuing of business licences (no business in the PRC is allowed to operate without such licence). When it comes to the conversion of foreign exchange into CNY or the cross-border transfer of funds, the State Administration for Foreign Exchange (SAFE) is the key regulator. If state-owned assets are involved, the State-owned Assets Supervision and Administration Commission (SASAC) and the Ministry of Finance (MOF) are the relevant regulators. Several industry regulators become relevant when investments fall within their scope of authority.

2.4.1 NDRC Approval or Record-Filing

[55] In the past, most foreign investment projects (both greenfield and M&A) were subject to NDRC approval, but this changed with the introduction of the *2014 NDRC Approval Rules*, while the *2017 NDRC Approval Rules* provide for further

[8] *2014 Insurance Equity Interest Measures*.

[9] Article1(2) *2019 Improving the Use of Foreign Investment Circular*.

relaxation.[10] Under these new rules, NDRC approval is only required for foreign investment projects if the relevant industry is listed in (a) the *Foreign Investment Negative List* (*see* section 2.1.1 'The Foreign Investment Negative List'),[11] or (b) sections 1-10 of the *Domestic Catalogue* (*see* [29]). Any foreign investment that does not fall within these categories only requires a record-filing with NDRC.[12] In practice, however, for many projects, no such record-filing is made, while foreign investors still manage to get all other approvals described below and obtain a business licence for their FIEs (this is mainly true for companies in the service and trade industry and for smaller projects that require relatively little investment). The reason for this is that the authorities in charge of other relevant approvals and granting the business licence carry out their work independently from NDRC. However, failure to complete the record-filing with NDRC may cause problems if the FIE, later on, intends to increase its investment or invests in projects that are subject to NDRC approval.

[56] NDRC approval needs to be sought at the central government level, at the provincial level or with the local authorities. The higher the level of approval, the more time and effort the process is expected to take. All projects in the *restricted category* of the *Foreign Investment Catalogue* with a value of at least USD2bn also need to be filed with the State Council, which is China's highest legislative organ. Investments in the *restricted* category require central government approval if these are at least USD300m, while below that threshold, provincial-level approval must be obtained. The relevant approval authority for each of the industries mentioned in sections 1-10 of the *Domestic Catalogue* is specified in this catalogue itself.[13]

[57] A foreign investor seeking NDRC approval needs to submit a project application report that includes basic information on the project and the foreign investor, an analysis of the utilization of resources and the impact on the environment and a social and economic impact analysis. In case of an M&A project, additional information needs to be provided on the acquisition details, the financing thereof, the business operations and any arrangement on the use of proceeds by the seller.[14] Other information to be submitted includes incorporation documents, financial statements, bank letters regarding creditworthiness and site-related opinions (e.g., an environmental impact report). Like most approval procedures in China, NDRC has the freedom to require any additional documents as it deems fit.[15]

[58] The criteria applied by NDRC when deciding whether to grant approval are:

[10] The *2014 NDRC Approval Rules* were amended in the same year by the *2014 NDRC Approval Rules Amendment*. Note that under the old rules, NDRC approval was in practice not always sought nor enforced by authorities (including NDRC itself).

[11] In the *2017 NDRC Approval Rules*, approval for *encouraged* industries with restrictions has been removed, but given the new *Foreign Investment Negative List*, it is expected that *encouraged* industries with restrictions still require approval, since these are included in the *Foreign Investment Negative List* and, therefore, are classified as *restricted*.

[12] Articles I, II *2017 NDRC Approval Rules*.

[13] Article I *2017 NDRC Approval Rules*.

[14] Article 8 *2014 NDRC Approval Rules*.

[15] Article 10 *2014 NDRC Approval Rules*.

(a) compliance with PRC laws and regulations (including the *Foreign Investment Negative List* and industry-specific rules)[16];
(b) compliance with national or regional development plans;
(c) whether resources are to be developed reasonably and utilized efficiently;
(d) no negative effects on national security or ecological safety; and
(e) no material impact on the public interest.[17]

[59] NDRC should decide on the application within twenty working days from its acceptance thereof, and such a deadline can be extended with an additional ten working days.[18] Note that the authorities will decide when an application is complete and thus accepted, and so, in practice, the application can take much longer. NDRC is supposed to engage a qualified advisory body within four working days from acceptance of the application to advise it on the matter; NDRC is also allowed to solicit the opinion of the public for projects that may materially affect public interests and certain experts for significant projects.[19]

[60] There are only a few reports of projects rejected by NDRC. One of them was Arcelor Mittal's attempt to become the largest shareholder of Valin Steel Tube & Wire Co. Ltd. NDRC rejected the transaction because it deemed that the relevant steel industry policy did not allow a foreign investor to purchase a controlling stake, after which Arcelor Mittal amended the transaction structure and became the second-largest shareholder.

[61] As mentioned above, foreign investment projects that do not require NDRC approval only require a simple record-filing. The documents for such record-filing are quite straightforward and include, for example, the basic particulars of the parties involved, their corporate registrations and a letter of intent on the nature of the investment. Should the record-filing not be accepted, the relevant authority is required to issue a written opinion or explanation within seven working days. In practice, such rejection should only occur if the project breaches PRC laws and regulations (e.g., non-compliance with the *Foreign Investment Negative List*).[20]

2.4.2 MOFCOM Approval or Record-Filing

[62] The incorporation or acquisition (including subscribing for new equity) of a PRC legal entity by a foreign investor, or the merger of an FIE with another PRC legal entity, requires approval from or a record-filing with MOFCOM.[21] Together

[16] Note that the *2017 NDRC Approval Rules* still refer to the abolished *Foreign Investment Catalogue* and have not yet been formally amended to reflect the introduction of the *Foreign Investment Negative List*. However, it is generally expected that NDRC will refer to the *Foreign Investment Negative List* when deciding whether or not to grant investment approval.

[17] Article 16 *2014 NDRC Approval Rules*.

[18] Article 15 *2014 NDRC Approval Rules*.

[19] Article 14 *2014 NDRC Approval Rules*.

[20] Articles 18–20 *2014 NDRC Approval Rules*; Art. II *2017 NDRC Approval Rules*.

[21] Exceptions are Foreign-Invested Partnerships (section 'Foreign Invested Partnership (FIP)') and Representative Offices (section 'Representative Office (RO)').

with the NDRC approval process set out above, MOFCOM approval or record-filing is usually considered one of the key steps for any foreign investment project (unless the approval of an industry regulator comes instead of MOFCOM approval, *see* section 2.4.4 'Industry Regulator Approvals' below).

[63] Until October 2016, MOFCOM approval was required for *all* foreign investment (unless an industry regulator has such authority). This changed with the *2016 FIE Filing Decision*, which replaced the approval requirement with a record-filing system for the incorporation of, and subsequent changes to (e.g., mergers, acquisitions, share issuances, increase of registered capital), Foreign-Invested Enterprises that operate outside the restricted industries of the *Foreign Investment Negative List* (in section 2.1.1 'The Foreign Investment Negative List' we explained that this list includes all *prohibited* and *restricted* industries). This is considered a milestone in China's foreign investment policy, since removing the burdensome and time-consuming MOFCOM approval requirement significantly simplifies foreign investment in non-restricted industries.[22]

[64] If a transaction involves any restricted industry that is included in the *Foreign Investment Negative List*, MOFCOM approval is still required,[23] and at application, an enterprise must confirm whether such restrictions apply.[24]

[65] Unlike the NDRC approval process, where the same rules apply for greenfield and M&A investments, no uniform set of regulations exists for the MOFCOM approval and record-filing process. Not only do different rules apply to greenfield and M&A but also each type of M&A transaction is governed by another set of rules. For example, different rules apply if the target is owned by domestic or foreign shareholders, if it is listed or if it enters into a merger.

[66] Given that different laws apply, we will describe the MOFCOM approval and record-filing process in more detail when we discuss the different types of investment. In Chapter 3 'Business Vehicles', we will set out this process for greenfield operations, and in Chapter 4 'Mergers & Acquisitions', for private M&A. Below, we will limit ourselves to making some brief general observations.

[67] First of all, it is not yet clear whether anything will change after the *Foreign Investment Law* becomes effective in January 2020. One could argue that since the law promises national treatment for industries outside the *Foreign Investment Negative List* (*see* [117] below), no special record-filing should be required for those industries, but it remains to be seen whether this will indeed be implemented.

[68] Until then, each incorporation, issuance of equity, acquisition or merger that involves foreign investors, regardless of its scale, industry or proposed activities, is subject to approval by, or a record-filing with, central MOFCOM or its local commission of commerce at provincial, municipal or district level. At which level

[22] *2016 Negative List Announcement*; Arts 2, 5, 6 *2016 FIE Filing Measures*; *2016 FIE Filing Decision*.

[23] Note that strategic investments in listed companies (*see* [96]) also still require MOFCOM approval under the *2005 Foreign Strategic Investment Measures*, even if the relevant industry is outside the *Foreign Investment Negative List*.

[24] *2019 Foreign-Invested Registration Opinions*, Art. 4.

approval needs to be sought, or a record-filing has to be made, depends on the location of the legal entity, the type of industry and the total amount of the investment. The higher the level of the authority whose approval is required, the more complicated and time-consuming the process usually will be. Generally speaking, investments in the *2019 Catalogue of Industries for Encouraged Foreign Investment* that have a transaction value of less than USD300m and those projects in *restricted* sectors with a transaction value of less than USD50m can be submitted to a local bureau of MOFCOM, while larger transactions should be approved by central MOFCOM.[25]

[69] In case MOFCOM *approval* is required, MOFCOM will carry out a substantive review of all application documents and basically check whether:

(a) the proposed business activity may be conducted by a foreign investor (i.e., compliance with the *Foreign Investment Negative List*);
(b) the compliance with industry-specific restrictions (*see* section 2.3 'Industry-Specific Restrictions' above) and whether industry regulator approval (if any) has been obtained (*see* section 2.4.4 'Industry Regulator Approvals' below);
(c) all formalities for the specific transaction (e.g., incorporation, merger, acquisition or issuance of new equity) have been met; and
(d) the investment generally complies with PRC laws.

If there are no objections, MOFCOM will issue an approval letter for the transaction.

[70] In case only a *record-filing* with MOFCOM is required, this filing can be submitted online at the competent MOFCOM department. MOFCOM will check if the filing is complete and accurate and whether the relevant transaction indeed only requires a record-filing. If there are no issues, MOFCOM will accept the record-filing online within three business days, and the applicant may collect a record-filing receipt thereafter. If the transaction falls outside the scope of the record-filing framework (e.g., the relevant industry is on the *Foreign Investment Negative List*), the filing will be rejected, while if the filing is deemed incomplete or inaccurate, the applicant will be granted a one-time fifteen business-day period to supplement the application.[26]

[71] One of the new, burdensome features of the record-filing system introduced in 2016 is that the *ultimate controller* of the Foreign-Invested Enterprise needs to be disclosed as part of the filing, and if this controller changes, the filing needs to be updated. According to MOFCOM, an ultimate controller is a person who, directly or indirectly, controls the FIE through shares, contracts, trust or any other method.[27] Note that it is only possible to report a listed company, natural person, governmental organization or international organization as the actual controller –

[25] *2010 FIE Approval Delegation Circular*; *2009 Foreign Investment Approval Circular*, *2009 FIHC Approval Circular*, *2008 Foreign Investment Licensing Circular*, *2008 FIE Approval Delegating Circular*.

[26] Articles 7, 11, 12 *2016 FIE Filing Measures*.

[27] Articles 5, 6 *2016 FIE Filing Measures*; Art. 5 *2016 FIE Filing Interpretation*.

i.e., it is *not* permitted to report a private company as the ultimate controller, which may create practical difficulties for many foreign investors. Fortunately, at least until the time of writing, most authorities show understanding of this point and seemingly apply some flexibility when asking for and reviewing the submitted information.

2.4.3 Business Licence and AMR Registration

[72] The new incorporation of a legal entity, or the transfer of equity (incl. merger of, or new subscription for), is completed when it is registered with SAMR or its local counterpart, the Administration of Market Regulation (AMR) in the locality where the target is registered, upon which a (new) business licence will be issued. In case only a record-filing with MOFCOM is required, both the *2016 FIE Filing Measures* (issued by MOFCOM) and the *2016 FIE Filing Circular* (issued by SAMR) allow for the possibility to obtain a business licence with AMR first and complete the record-filing with MOFCOM within thirty days thereafter, and this is becoming a standard practice.[28] While not in compliance with the legally established procedures, some local AMRs still require the record-filing receipt issued by MOFCOM to be submitted to them *before* they are willing to issue the business licence.

[73] Upon the issuance of a business licence, a new entity is duly incorporated, while any acquisition, merger or subscription for equity is deemed completed upon the registration, thereof, with the AMR. This step – although an important one – is usually only a formality and does not involve a substantive review of application documents (except that AMRs regularly require changes to proposed business scopes; *see* [198] below). Note that the AMR process is not considered a restriction on foreign investment (the scope of this chapter) since domestic investors need to go through the same process.

2.4.4 Industry Regulator Approvals

[74] Besides general investment approval from, or a record-filing with, NDRC and MOFCOM, many foreign investments also require industry regulator approval. The main goal of such approval is ensuring compliance with industry-specific restrictions (*see* section 2.3 'Industry-Specific Restrictions'). If there are no industry-specific regulations, usually, no approval from an industry regulator is required.

[75] Some of the key PRC industry regulators include:

(a) China Banking Regulatory Commission (CBRC);
(b) China Insurance Regulatory Commission (CIRC);
(c) China Securities Regulatory Commission (CSRC);
(d) Ministry of Industry and Information Technology (MIIT) for the telecom sector (including e-commerce);

[28] Article 11 *2016 FIE Filing Measures*; Art. 3 *2016 FIE Filing Circular*.

(e) Ministry of Housing and Urban-Rural Development for construction/engineering;
(f) *Ministry of Transport* for road/railway transport;
(g) *Ministry of Health* for medical institutions; and
(h) MOFCOM – besides its role as general regulator for foreign investment, MOFCOM also acts as the industry regulator for several industries.

[76] Industry-regulator approval is usually connected to the general MOFCOM investment approval (or record-filing) in one of the following ways:

(1) The *industry regulator directly approves* the foreign investment, and no MOFCOM approval is required – examples are investments in banks, securities companies and representative offices of foreign law firms, where CBRC, CSRC and the *Ministry of Justice*, respectively approve the investment instead of MOFCOM.[29]
(2) *Pre-approval from the industry regulator* is required before submitting the foreign investment project to MOFCOM for approval – examples are investments in medical institutions and the telecom sector, which need to be pre-approved by the Ministry of Health and MIIT, respectively.[30]
(3) Only MOFCOM approval is required, but MOFCOM seeks the *opinion of the industry regulator*, which opinion MOFCOM usually follows, and which can also be other departments of MOFCOM if MOFCOM itself is the industry regulator – examples are construction engineering services (Ministry of Housing and Urban-Rural Development), distribution, retail, leasing and international freight forwarding (all MOFCOM).[31]
(4) *Post-approval from the industry regulator* is required after obtaining MOFCOM approval or making a record-filing with MOFCOM (and usually also after obtaining the business licence (section 2.4.3 'Business Licence and AMR Registration')) – examples are the food industry and hazardous waste (the Food and Drug Administration and the Ministry of Environmental Protection being the relevant regulators).[32]

[77] In the past few years, many industry-specific licences have changed from pre-approval to post-approval, meaning that foreign investors can complete the MOFCOM procedures and obtain their business licence first and apply for the industry-specific licence thereafter (these changes equally apply to domestic investors, except that they don't need to go through the MOFCOM procedures). In these industries, it is now much easier and faster to establish a company and start trading since there is no longer any need to wait for the industry regulator's approval

[29] Article 7 *2006 Foreign-invested Banks Regulations*; Art. 13 *2002 Foreign-invested Securities Companies Rules*; Art. 6 *2001 Regulations on Foreign Law Firms*; Art. 12 *2003 Sino-foreign Education Regulations*.

[30] Articles 10–13 *2000 FIE Medical Institutions Interim Measures*; Arts 12, 13, 15 *2008 FIE Telecom Enterprises Provisions (revised in 2016)*.

[31] Article 7 *2002 FIE Construction Measures*; *2005 FIE Leasing Measures*; Art. 11 *2005 FIE Freight Transportation Measures*.

[32] *2009 Food Safety Regulations (revised in 2016)*; *2004 Hazardous Waste Measures (revised in 2016)*.

(except that regulated activities may obviously only be carried out after the relevant licence has been obtained).[33]

2.4.5 National Security Review

[78] Like several other jurisdictions, China has established a national security review system for acquisitions by foreign investors in sensitive industries. If this review is required (not often the case), it will be conducted prior to the other approval procedures described above. Upon completion of the review, Chinese authorities may block a transaction, or require its terms to be amended, if such a transaction has impact on China's national security, economic stability or social order.

[79] The national security review system came into effect in 2011 when the State Council set out its general principles in the *2011 Security Review Notice*. Detailed rules followed later that year when MOFCOM issued the *2011 Security Review Provisions*. In 2015, the *National Security Law* came into force, which provides a high-level legal framework for the national security review and defines national security as 'the absence of international and domestic threats to the State's power to govern, sovereignty, unity and territorial integrity, the welfare of the people, sustainable development of economy and society, and other significant national interests, and the country's ability to safeguard security on a continuous basis.'[34]

[80] The *National Security Law* requires the establishment of a security review system for foreign investment that has a potential impact on national security,[35] but the wording is general, and the law itself does not provide detailed regulations for the implementation of such system. The *2011 Security Review Notice* does provide detailed implementing rules, but these are limited to M&A transactions.

[81] Two types of M&A transactions by foreign investors are currently subject to review under the *2011 Security Review Notice*: (i) transactions in the military sector, including target companies adjacent to key or sensitive military sites or other targets related to China's national defence, and (ii) transactions resulting in a foreign investor 'acquiring actual control' over a domestic target which has 'bearing on national security' and is active in the area of 'important' agricultural products, energy and resources, infrastructure, transport services, technology or equipment manufacturing.[36]

[82] 'Acquiring actual control' means acquiring: (i) more than 50% of the equity or voting rights, (ii) significant influence over the shareholders meeting or board, or

[33] *See*, for example, the *2015 Business License First Circular* and the *2015 Industry Licenses Adjustment*.

[34] Article 2 *National Security Law*.

[35] Article 59 *National Security Law*.

[36] Article 1(1) *2011 Security Review Notice*. In addition, Arts 20–25, 30–32 of the *National Security Law* specifically mention the following industries as being important to national security: finance, resources and energy, food safety, culture, cybersecurity, advanced technology, network and information technologies, nuclear power, environmental protection and the exploration of outer space, international waters and polar regions.

(iii) actual control over operational, financial, personnel or technological affairs.[37] It is not clear what '"bearing on national security" and "important"' means, which gives the authorities a significant degree of discretion. Both equity and asset transactions fall under the scope of the review,[38] and the substance of a transaction determines whether it is subject to review, as avoiding the national security review through creative structuring (e.g., VIE, trust, nominee holding structures) is explicitly prohibited.[39]

[83] For foreign investments in the Free Trade Zones, a more detailed national security review system was introduced by the *2015 FTZ Security Review Circular* that specifies the scope of national security review as 'investments in military industry, military support and other areas which relate to national defence security, as well as surrounding areas of key, sensitive military facilities; investments in key agricultural products, key energies and resources, key infrastructure, key transportation services, key culture, key information technology products and services, key technologies, key equipment manufacturing etc. which relate to national security and obtain the actual controlling stake of the investee enterprises'.[40] It also clarifies that any review of a foreign investment in an FTZ shall be carried out pursuant to the *2011 Security Review Notice*.

[84] There are three ways to initiate a national security review: (1) a voluntary filing by the foreign investor,[41] (2) a local department of NDRC or MOFCOM reporting the transaction to central NDRC or MOFCOM (local MOFCOM usually becomes aware of a transaction when it is submitted to it for general investment approval or record-filing), or (3) upon request by a third party (e.g., concerned government authorities, industrial associations, competitors, upstream/downstream businesses).[42] It is no surprise that very few foreign investors have self-reported their transactions.

[85] There are hardly any reports that local authorities or interested third parties have initiated national security reviews, but in August 2019, Yonghui Supermarkets (a Chinese-owned company with 20% foreign investment) announced that it had received a letter from NDRC requesting it to submit its intended acquisition of a controlling stake in the Zhongbai Group for a national security review. This followed a notice from April 2019 that NDRC has taken over all national security review responsibilities from MOFCOM due to an 'adjustment of ministerial functions'.[43]

[37] Article 1(3) *2011 Security Review Notice*.

[38] Article 1(2) *2011 Security Review Notice*.

[39] Article 9 *2011 Security Review Provisions*.

[40] *Article 1(1) 2015 FTZ Security Review Circular*.

[41] If a foreign investor expects issues in this respect, it may also informally consult with MOFCOM prior to a transaction, although such consultation does not have legal and binding effect (Art. 4 *2011 Security Review Provisions*).

[42] Articles 1–3 *2011 Security Review Provisions*.

[43] *2019 NDRC Notice No. 4*.

[86] When NDRC receives an application for national security review and deems it complete,[44] it has fifteen business-days to decide whether such review indeed needs to be conducted. If there is no response from NDRC within that period, the transaction may automatically proceed without further review.[45] In the event NDRC determines that a security review is required, it shall forward the transaction for a substantive review to a joint ministerial panel consisting of representatives from NDRC, MOFCOM and other relevant ministries and agencies. This committee shall solicit views from relevant authorities, and if there are no concerns, the transaction shall be approved within forty business days. If there are national security concerns, a special review shall be initiated that may take sixty business days. If the committee decides that the file needs to be submitted to the State Council, the process may take even longer.[46]

[87] The criteria used to evaluate transactions are their impact on: (i) national security, including domestic production and service capacity, and related equipment and facilities needed for national security purposes, (ii) China's economic stability, (iii) China's social order, and (iv) China's R&D capacity of critical technology related to national security.[47] There is no further guidance as how to interpret these criteria.

2.4.6 State-Owned Assets

[88] Foreign investors are, in principle, allowed to acquire PRC state-owned equity and assets (except in industries where foreign investment is prohibited). In order to prevent state-owned assets from being sold below their true value, the PRC government has put several safeguards in place. For example, the value of assets need to be appraised by a qualified institute, approval is required from State-owned Assets Supervision and Administration Commission (SASAC) or its local counterpart and public bids need to be solicited through a so-called property rights exchange (resulting in an auction or bid-process in case of multiple interested parties). *State-owned Assets Law* and the *2016 SOE Trading Measures* are the key pieces of legislation in this respect. These rules do not distinguish between foreign and domestic investors,[48] so there are, in principle, no restrictions specifically aimed at foreign investors (the scope of this chapter). We will discuss the acquisition of state-owned assets more extensively in Chapter 4 'Mergers & Acquisitions' (section 4.7 'Acquisition of State-Owned Assets').

[44] Note that MOFCOM has broad discretion to require additional documents before it deems an application complete (Art. 5(9) *2011 Security Review Provisions*).

[45] Article 6 *2011 Security Review Provisions*.

[46] Article 4(3) *2011 Security Review Notice*; Art. 7-8 *2011 Security Review Provisions*.

[47] Art. 2 *2011 Security Review Notice*.

[48] Except that Art. 57 *State-Owned Assets Law* states that any transfer of state-owned assets to an overseas investor should not compromise national security and public interest.

2.4.7 Merger Control

[89] Like in many other jurisdictions, China has implemented a merger control system that requires transactions above certain notification thresholds to be submitted to MOFCOM for anti-monopoly clearance. The *2008 PRC Anti-Monopoly Law* does not distinguish between foreign and domestic investors, so even though foreign investors do need to obtain merger clearance from MOFCOM for certain transactions, they should not be in a more unfavourable position than their domestic peers. We will discuss the merger clearance process in detail in section 4.8.6 'Merger Control'.

2.5 Acquisition of Listed Shares

[90] The acquisition of listed shares falls outside the scope of this publication, but in this section, we will briefly highlight the relevant restrictions on foreign investment.

[91] Mainland China has two stock markets, one in Shanghai and one in Shenzhen. Both have an A-share market with shares denominated in CNY and a B-share market with shares traded in foreign currency (USD in Shanghai, Hong Kong Dollar in Shenzhen). Traditionally, foreign investors were only allowed to purchase B-shares, while A-shares were off-limits (a listed company can issue both A-shares and B-shares).

[92] B-shares usually trade at a fairly large discount compared to A-shares, given the lack of liquidity on this market. This is despite the fact that since 2001, domestic investors have also been able to buy B-shares. Furthermore, often only a limited class of B-shares is available, giving foreign investors little control over these companies.

[93] The A-share market first opened in 2002 to certain licensed foreign institutional investors who qualified under the Qualified Foreign Institutional Investors (QFII) scheme. These institutional investors are permitted to acquire A-shares, with a cap of 10% per PRC listed company, while the total foreign investment in each listed company may not exceed 30%. QFIIs send their funds to China in foreign currency (usually USD), where they are converted into CNY prior to acquiring A-shares.[49]

[94] Since late 2011, foreign institutional investors can also qualify under the Renminbi Qualified Foreign Institutional Investors (RQFII) scheme. This is quite similar to the QFII scheme with the key difference that foreign investors may directly

[49] *2006 QFII Measures*.

use CNY legally obtained outside China to invest in the A-share market, so there is no need to send in foreign currency and convert this within China.[50]

[95] In October 2014, the A-share market further opened up through *Shanghai-Hong Kong Stock Connect*. Stock Connect allows foreign investors to acquire certain eligible A-shares on the Shanghai stock exchange through qualified Hong Kong brokers (and vice-versa Chinese investors may acquire Hong Kong listed shares in Shanghai).[51] In December 2016, a similar system was implemented between the Hong Kong and Shenzhen stock markets.

[96] Outside the QFII, RQFII and Stock Connect schemes, *any* foreign investor who meets certain qualifications (*e.g.*, having itself at least USD100m worth of assets, or having at least USD500m under management) is, after obtaining approval and subject to certain restrictions (e.g., a three-year lock-up), allowed to carry out a block trade of at least 10% in a PRC listed company as a strategic investment.[52]

[97] It is possible for a foreign investor to carry out such strategic investment by means of a public takeover (provided full foreign ownership is permitted in the relevant industry). Like in most jurisdictions, the PRC also regulates public takeovers. Even though all the usual restrictions on foreign investment apply to a public takeover, the PRC public takeover regulations as such do not differentiate between foreign and domestic investors.[53]

2.6 Foreign Exchange Restrictions

[98] The Chinese national currency – the Chinese Yuan (CNY), also often referred to as the Renminbi (RMB) (literally translated as the 'people's money') – is not freely convertible. As a general rule, foreign currency may not be used within Mainland China (save for some limited exceptions), while all transactions involving foreign exchange are, to a certain extent, controlled by the government.[54] Initially, China established strict foreign exchange controls to prevent capital from leaving the country, but in recent years it has also used these controls to restrict the inflow of foreign funds to prevent its economy from overheating. Foreign investors should, therefore, carefully consider these restrictions for each of their projects, unless they already have local currency available in China from existing businesses.

[50] Late 2011 the programme started on a trial basis with a small quota, which quota was significantly increased in 2013 when also new rules were issued, while further rules were issued in 2016, *see* the *2013 RQFII Implementation Provisions* and the *2016 RQFII Measures*.

[51] *2016 Stock Connect Provisions*.

[52] *2005 Foreign Strategic Investment Measures*.

[53] *2002 Public Takeover Measures (last revised in 2014)*. Art. 4 and 89 *2002 Public Takeover Measures* do make it clear that foreign investors carrying out a public takeover are subject to PRC law, and still need to comply with all applicable foreign direct investment regulations, such as the *2005 Foreign Strategic Investment Measures* mentioned above.

[54] Art. 2, 8 *2008 Forex Control Regulations*.

[99] The key regulator with respect to foreign exchange controls is SAFE, while the People's Bank of China (PBOC) also plays a significant role on a macroeconomic level. SAFE has delegated many of its powers to designated financial institutions who enforce the day-to-day compliance with foreign exchange regulations.[55] This means that the key question for many cross-border payments to and from China is whether the bank is willing to process them, and if so, which supporting documents the bank requires.

[100] An important aspect of foreign exchange regulations is the distinction between the *current account* and the *capital account*. The current account relates to ordinary course of business transactions, including payments for the sale of goods, services, licensing, leasing and dividends.[56] For these items, currency can, in principle, be converted freely upon providing the bank with evidence that the underlying transactions are genuine (e.g., contracts, invoices) and that relevant taxes (if any) have been paid.[57] The capital account relates to equity transfers, increase and reduction of equity, foreign direct investments, foreign investment in securities, foreign loans and cross-border guarantees.[58] Control over these transactions is much stricter than current account items, and transactions generally require approval or registration.[59]

[101] Our focus will be on payments going through the capital account since these are typically relevant to foreign investors when setting up greenfield operations or acquiring domestic targets. We will discuss the relevant foreign exchange rules for greenfield operations in Chapter 3 'Business Vehicles' and the rules for cross-border payments in relation to changes in equity holdings in Chapter 4 'Mergers & Acquisitions'. Below, we limit ourselves to a brief description of the main features of these regulations.

[102] For greenfield operations and equity subscriptions in existing companies, the main foreign exchange issue is the injection of capital into Foreign-Invested Enterprise and the subsequent conversion into CNY. Traditionally, capital contributions were always made in foreign currency, but onshore CNY income may also be reinvested (e.g., dividends received in CNY); moreover, lawfully obtained offshore CNY may now be used as well, and this is gaining in popularity.[60]

[103] The *Foreign Investment Law* stipulates in general terms that foreign investors may freely remit into or out of China, in CNY or any other foreign currency, their

[55] Art. 4 *2014 Forex Settlement by Banks Measures*; Art. 7, 24 *2008 Forex Control Regulations*; art. 2 *1996 Forex Settlement Regulation.*

[56] Art. 52(3) *2008 Forex Control Regulations.*

[57] Art. 5, 12 *2008 Forex Control Regulations.*

[58] Article 52(4) *2008 Forex Control Regulations.*

[59] Articles 21-23 *2008 Forex Control Regulations.*

[60] Article 25 *1990 WFOE Implementing Rules*, Art. 2 *2012 Forex FDI Circular*; Art. 1 *2013 RMB Direct Investment Announcement.*

capital contributions, profits, capital gains, income from asset disposals, intellectual property royalties and lawfully obtained compensation, indemnity or liquidation income. However, it remains to be seen whether it will become easier to remit funds into and out of China when this law becomes effective in January 2020.

[104] Besides contributing capital, many foreign investors prefer to fund their Chinese subsidiaries with shareholder loans from outside China. Foreign debt is, however, subject to strict caps (*see* section 3.5.2 'Financing with Foreign Loans'), and many foreign investors are unpleasantly surprised by the limited flexibility they have in salvaging temporary cash-flow shortages with shareholder loans.[61] Cross-border guarantees are also regulated, but since 2014, these are no longer subject to quota and SAFE approval (only registration with SAFE for certain guarantees).[62]

[105] Conversion of funds received by Foreign-Invested Enterprise as registered capital or foreign debt is only allowed for activities within such company's business scope and is subject to several restrictions (e.g., no investment in securities, no purchase of real estate that is not for own use, and no extension of loans to non-affiliated parties)[63] and varying procedural requirements enforced by the banks. However, the previous rule that registered capital could not be converted and used for investment (incl. establishment of a Chinese subsidiary) was recently cancelled, which should give FIE's more flexibility in corporate structuring within China.[64]

[106] With respect to equity transfers, foreign exchange regulations mainly play a role if a PRC company is acquired by a foreign buyer from a domestic seller. The foreign buyer will usually pay the purchase price in foreign currency, which subsequently needs to be converted by the domestic seller into CNY. Previously, such conversion required SAFE approval, but this system has been abolished in the course of 2012 and 2013.[65] Until June 2015, registration of the transaction with SAFE was still required, but this has been delegated to the designated banks who will have to ensure compliance with the relevant foreign exchange regulations.[66]

2.7 Pilot Free Trade Zones

[107] In late 2013, in an effort to further lift restrictions on foreign investment, the Chinese government officially launched the China (Shanghai) Pilot Free-Trade Zone (Shanghai FTZ). The basic idea of the zone is to test liberalization policies in a controlled environment and, when successful, to roll them out nationwide.

[61] *2017 Foreign Debt Notice*; *2003 Foreign Debt Management Measures*; *2013 Foreign Debt Registration Guidelines*; *2015 Forex FDI Circular*.

[62] *2014 Cross-border Guarantee Provisions*.

[63] Article 4 *2016 Capital Account Reform Circular* (exceptions apply to the restrictions mentioned).

[64] Article 2,4 *2019 SAFE Notice on Cross-border Trade and Investment*.

[65] *2012 Forex FDI Circular* and *2013 Forex FDI Provisions*.

[66] Article 2, 3 *2015 Forex FDI Circular*.

[108] The original Shanghai FTZ covered an area of 29 square kilometres that integrated four previously existing bonded zones in Shanghai (i.e., zones where already certain beneficial policies for foreign trade applied). Three other districts in Shanghai subsequently merged with the Shanghai FTZ, resulting in all companies registered in these districts immediately falling under the FTZ regime. In March 2015, the Chinese government formally approved the establishment of three new free trade zones in Tianjin, Guangdong and Fujian, where the model of the Shanghai FTZ is copied.[67] In 2016, it was announced by the PRC government that it has given approval for the establishment of seven additional free trade zones all over China and these were opened in 2017 (jointly, we refer to these free trade zones as the 'FTZ').

[109] The FTZs are not separate jurisdictions and all PRC laws and regulations apply unless set aside or amended by regulations specifically applicable to the FTZs. For several years the key benefit of the FTZs was that, in general, no approval for foreign investment is required, unless the industry is on the current *FTZ Negative List*.[68]

[110] Reform in the FTZs is not exclusively handled through the *FTZ Negative List*. Some specific industries have opened up by means of specific regulation. Examples are relaxed restrictions on foreign ownership in the value-added telecom services sector (e.g., e-commerce and call centres),[69] international shipping joint ventures[70] and medical institutions (and some of these measures were later rolled out nationwide).[71]

[111] In section 2.6 'Foreign Exchange Restrictions', we discussed that the CNY is neither freely convertible into other currencies nor can it be freely transferred in and out of China. The Shanghai FTZ has issued several initiatives to remove these restrictions. Multinational corporations established in the zone are, for example, allowed to set up a two-way CNY cash pooling system.[72] Several banks already offer such system, which enables these corporations to integrate their onshore CNY cash flow (generated throughout China) with their global cash pool (subject to certain restrictions). Saint-Gobain, Dover Corporation (both with HSBC), Sonepar (with *RBS*) and Roche (with Citi) are reportedly among the first multinationals who have put such cash pooling systems in place. After the successful implementation within the Shanghai FTZ, a similar cash pooling programme was later made available nationwide.[73]

[112] The Shanghai FTZ also sees all kind of other reform initiatives. An interesting one is the FTZ Court of Arbitration set up by the Shanghai International Economic Trade Arbitration Commission (SHIAC) in October 2013 and SHIAC's

[67] *2015 Tianjin, Guangdong and Fujian FTZ Circular.*
[68] *2019 FTZ Negative List.*
[69] *2014 Shanghai FTZ Telecom Opinions*; *2014 Shanghai FTZ Telecom Notice.*
[70] *2014 Shanghai FTZ Shipping Announcement.*
[71] *2013 Shanghai FTZ WFOE Medical Institutions Tentative Measures.*
[72] *2014 Shanghai FTZ Cash Pooling Notice.*
[73] *2014 Cash Pooling Circular*; *2015 Cash Pooling Notice.*

special FTZ arbitration rules which became effective in May 2014 (last amendment in 2015). These FTZ rules will apply if contracting parties have opted for SHIAC arbitration and if: (a) there is a nexus between the FTZ and the parties, or (b) the parties explicitly opted for their application (even if there is no relation to the FTZ). The special rules include the possibility for interim measures, flexibility to agree on rules of evidence, consolidation with other arbitration cases, joinder of third parties and summary proceedings for small cases (below CNY1 000 000).

[113] Also on the administrative front, there have been improvements in the Shanghai FTZ. The authorities in the zone have set up a one-stop filing agency where investors can file several regulatory applications at once (e.g., NDRC, MOFCOM, tax authorities, customs), making the investment process smoother than outside the zone (although some policies were subsequently rolled out nationwide as well). The customs authorities have also streamlined their processes, including the possibility for paperless filings of certain details.

[114] In 2015, to balance the fewer restrictions on foreign investment in the FTZs, the national security review system (*see* section 2.4.5 'National Security Review' above) was made more strict in the FTZs compared to the rest of China. The nationwide security review is limited to M&A transactions only, but in the FTZs *any* foreign investment can nowadays be subject to a national security review. Otherwise, the review process in the FTZs is basically the same as under the nationwide system, except that *important culture* and *important information technology products and services* have been added to the list of sensitive industries where foreign investment may trigger a review.[74]

2.8 The Foreign Investment Law

[115] In March 2019, China formally promulgated the *Foreign Investment Law*. Under this law, much of what we described above will change in the coming years. In particular, the specific laws for the Wholly Foreign-Owned Enterprises, Equity Joint Ventures and Cooperative Joint Ventures will lose effect, which means that from a procedural and legal perspective, companies with foreign investment will largely be treated in the same way as their counterparts with only Chinese investment.

[116] The *Foreign Investment Law* applies to all investment activity directly or indirectly conducted by foreign natural persons, companies or other organizations whether through new projects, through the acquisition of equity or shares or otherwise. The reference to 'indirectly' suggests that this may include VIEs (*see* section 2.1.4 'Circumventing Restrictions: Variable Interest Entities (VIEs)' above); however, the *2015 Draft Foreign Investment Law* was much more explicit on this point, subjecting the control of a domestic enterprise by means of a contract or trust to the same approval or record-filing procedures as regular companies with foreign

[74] *2015 FTZ Security Review Circular*.

investment.[75] One interpretation has been that VIE structures with foreign controllers will *not* be subject to the *Foreign Investment Law* related restrictions (in particular, the negative lists) though for now this is left open to interpretation.

[117] Besides establishing a level playing field in procedures, the *Foreign Investment Law* contains numerous articles on how foreign investment will be subject to national treatment. For example, national policies supporting the development of enterprises will apply equally to companies with foreign and domestic investment; foreign-funded companies can participate in government procurement activities; and they can procure financing through public offerings of shares, corporate bonds and other securities.

[118] The *Foreign Investment Law* specifically refers to the mechanism of negative lists as the only means to restrict foreign investment in 'specific fields' – the law is very explicit about the principle that domestic investment and foreign investment shall be treated uniformly in other fields.[76] Moreover, where separate licensing requirements apply, the supervising authorities should apply the same rules and procedures as for companies with domestic investment.[77]

[119] While emphasizing national treatment, the *Foreign Investment Law* allows for preferential treatment for foreign investment as well, mainly in three ways. First, China may adopt laws and administrative regulations to offer preferential treatment to foreign investments, so as to encourage and guide foreign investment in specific industries as per China's economic and social developmental needs.[78] Second, any commitments that local authorities make to attract foreign investors shall continue to be legally binding.[79] In the past, local governments and relevant departments would offer preferential treatment to attract much-wanted foreign investment to their area, a practice that is now set to continue. And finally, where industries are listed in the negative lists, but preferential access is offered through an international treaty or agreement (e.g., CEPA, *see* section 2.1.3 'Preferential Treatment for Hong Kong, Macao and Taiwan Investors'), then such preferential treatment will continue to apply as well.[80]

[120] The final article of the *Foreign Investment Law* may, at least for now, be the most important article: while the specific laws and implementing rules for the Wholly Foreign-Owned Enterprises, Equity Joint Ventures and Cooperative Joint Ventures will lose effect upon enactment of this law, companies with foreign investment that are established before 1 January 2020 may retain their organization form for another five years (the *Transition Period*) – subject to further implementing rules to be issued in due time. This means that any change for existing foreign-invested companies is not immediate, but it also creates uncertainty for the future. In the

[75] *2015 Draft Foreign Investment Law*, Art. 14.

[76] *Foreign Investment Law*, Art. 4.

[77] *Foreign Investment Law*, Art. 30.

[78] *Foreign Investment Law*, Art. 14.

[79] *Foreign Investment Law*, Art. 25.

[80] *Foreign Investment Law*, Art. 4.

case of companies with only foreign investment, few problems are expected as corporate governance structures will remain broadly the same. For joint ventures, however, the transition could have a much greater impact as it will be an opportunity for the parties to such joint venture to negotiate new terms and conditions when transitioning to a new corporate governance structure (*see* section 3.3.2 'Equity Joint Venture (EJV)' below).

[121] The above concerns have not been resolved with the *2019 Draft FDI Implementing Regulation*, which is the first draft of the rules that is designed to provide further guidance on how the Foreign Investment Law is to be implemented. The rules reassure that the profit distribution arrangements of joint ventures established under previous laws shall not be affected by the adjustment of the organizational structure, which should be completed within six months of the Transition Period, but they are silent on how decision-making should be adjusted if the involved parties do not reach a new agreement. Rather, they specifically provide that detailed measures for changes in organization forms and organization structures of existing FIE's will be issued in the future. [81]

2.9 Approval for Outbound M&A Transactions

[122] M&A transactions by Chinese companies outside of China also require PRC government approval or record-filing. The restrictions for such investments have been considerably relaxed over the past few years, and these days, in principle, only outbound investments in *sensitive countries, regions or industries* require MOFCOM and NDRC approval. All other outbound investments only require a record-filing with both MOFCOM and NDRC, the approval level depending on the investment amount flowing out from China.[82]

[123] *Sensitive countries and regions* have been defined as those countries or regions with whom China has no diplomatic relationships, which are subject to international sanctions, where a war or civil unrest is taking place, or where investment is restricted according to the international treaties and protocols concluded or acceded by China. *Sensitive industries* include cross-border exploration of water resources, research, production, maintenance and repair of weapons and equipment, news media, real estate, hotels, cinema, entertainment, sports club, setting up equity investment funds or investment platforms abroad without specific industrial projects and industries which affect the interests of more than one country (region).[83]

[124] A project exceeding USD300m requires a record-filing with central-level NDRC, which needs to be approved by NDRC by issuing a registration notice.

81 *2019 Draft FDI Implementing Regulation*, Art. 42.

82 Article 12 *Domestic Catalogue*; Arts 13–14 *2018 Outbound Investment Measures*; Art. 1 *2014 NDRC Approval Rules Amendment*; Art. 6 *2014 Outbound Investment Rules*

83 Article 7 *2014 Outbound Investment Rules*; Art. 13 *2018 Outbound Investment Measures; 2018 Catalogue of Sensitive Industries*.

NDRC has discretion to reject a transaction if it does not meet the 'policy of the State on overseas investments'.

[125] Previously, before carrying out any 'substantive work' (including signing a binding agreement, submitting a binding offer, or making a formal bid in an auction) on outbound transactions exceeding USD300m, a preliminary filing had to be made first and also accepted by a confirmation letter from NDRC, which – at its discretion – would only issue the confirmation letter if the investment met the 'policy of the State on overseas investments'.

[126] The good news is that in March 2018, the *2018 Outbound Investment Measures* took effect, relaxing the restrictions on outbound transactions. The key changes are:

(a) removal of the State Council's approval for sensitive transactions exceeding USD2bn (NDRC and MOFCOM approval is still required);
(b) NDRC's confirmation letter will no longer be required before carrying out *substantive work* on sensitive projects exceeding USD300m (instead, only a simple filing receipt is required, which should not be subject to NDRC's discretion and should be issued to the investor within seven working days upon the acceptance of application documents compliant with statutory forms[84]); and
(c) a letter of intent from the bank will no longer be required for projects that require NDRC approval.

[127] Notwithstanding the above new policies, the PRC government remains concerned about excessive capital outflow, which occurred, among others, through outbound M&A transactions. Banks, as the last point of control with respect to capital outflows, are, therefore, enhancing their checks with respect to the authenticity and compliance with outbound investment rules under the supervision of SAFE. Before any funds can be remitted out of China, banks typically require the source and purpose (utilization plan) of the investment capital, resolutions of the board of directors, the share purchase or investment contract or other proof with respect to the authenticity of the transaction to be submitted.[85]

3 BUSINESS VEHICLES

3.1 Introduction

[128] Business vehicles are obviously relevant when it comes to mergers and acquisitions, and in China a good understanding, thereof, is even more important. The first reason is that historically a distinction was made between entities with foreign

[84] Articles 30–31 *2018 Outbound Investment Measures.*
[85] Article 8 *2017 SAFE Notice on Promoting Foreign Exchange Control.*

investment and those with only domestic investors, and when a foreign investor acquired, or subscribed for, equity in a domestic-owned entity, such domestic-owned entity automatically converted into one of the legal forms available to foreign investors. These vehicles for foreign investors are also subject to several restrictions, which have a significant impact on how M&A transactions can be structured.

[129] Another reason that business vehicles are important in China is that PRC law has imposed limits on foreign ownership in several industries through the *Foreign Investment Negative List* (*see* 2.1.1 'The Foreign Investment Negative List' above), forcing foreign investors to co-invest with a Chinese joint-venture partner. The result is that many foreign investments in China are structured as greenfield projects, whereby Chinese and foreign investors jointly incorporate a new business vehicle.

[130] Foreign-Invested Enterprise (FIE) is the overall name for a *Chinese company* in which a foreign investor is allowed to invest. The following types of FIEs are available:

(a) Wholly Foreign-Owned Enterpris*e* (WFOE);
(b) Equity Joint Venture (EJV);
(c) Cooperative Joint Venture (CJV); and
(d) Foreign-Invested Company Limited by Shares (FICLS).

[131] For now, each of these FIE types remains governed by its own set of rules, including a law (which is promulgated by the State Council) and implementing rules (which are promulgated at the ministerial level) and certain rules that apply to all FIEs in general. The general provisions of the *Company Law* apply as well, unless there is a conflict with a specific law (though not any implementing rules, since the *Company Law* trumps such rules).

[132] However, when the *Foreign Investment Law* becomes effective on 1 January 2020 new FIEs can no longer be established, and instead foreign investors will have to incorporate one of the ordinary vehicles already available to domestic investors under the general framework of the *Company Law*: the *limited liability company* and the *company limited by shares*.

[133] In this chapter, we will, therefore, first set out the basics of the *Company Law* (section 3.2 'The Basics of PRC Company Law'), since this will be the new reality as of 2020, and also because the *Company Law* provides the general framework under which existing FIEs are regulated.

[134] Existing FIEs will be permitted to continue with their current corporate form during a five-year transition period, hence understanding FIEs, therefore, remains an important part of understanding China's legal landscape. We will discuss each different FIE in section 2.2 'Foreign-Invested Enterprises', after which we will separately address two important aspects that apply to FIEs in general: their incorporation and approval procedures (section 3.4 'Set-up and Approval of

Foreign-Invested Enterprises'), and their capitalization and financing (section 3.5 'Financing of Foreign-Invested Enterprises').

[135] At the end of this chapter (section 3.6 'Other Business Vehicles Available to Foreign Investors'), we will describe three other business vehicles available to foreign investors that are *not* considered FIEs: Representative Office (RO), Foreign-Invested Partnership (FIP), and the domestic subsidiary of an FIE. The RO is not an FIE, since it is not a separate legal person, the FIP is not an FIE because it is a partnership and not an enterprise and the domestic subsidiary is not considered an FIE because it only has domestic shareholders (which may be an FIE).

3.2 The Basics of PRC Company Law

[136] One is not permitted to carry on a business in China without a business licence.[86] A business licence is issued upon the incorporation of a legal entity (*see* section 3.4.5 'Business Licence and Post-approval Registrations') and specifies, amongst others, the entity's business scope. If certain business activities require a separate licence (section 2.3 'Industry-Specific Restrictions'), the authorities will only allow these activities to be included in the business scope if the relevant approvals have been obtained, or if the relevant industry licence can only be applied for after the business licence is granted ([76]), the business scope will state that the activities may only be carried out after the relevant licence has been obtained. The strategy to define a business scope as broad as possible (as is common in many other jurisdictions) often does not work in China due to these licence restrictions and the policies of local authorities. Chinese legal entities (including FIEs and the FIP) are prohibited from conducting any revenue-generating activities outside their business scope.[87]

[137] The *Company Law* provides for two different legal entities: the *limited liability company,* and the *company limited by shares*. When the *Foreign Investment Law* becomes effective in January 2020, foreign investors will be permitted to establish those two legal entities as well. Limited liability companies issue so-called *equity interests* (which are not shares) to their investors pro rata their contribution to the company's registered capital. Companies limited by shares issue individual *shares* and are, therefore, the only type of PRC legal entity that can get listed on a stock exchange. FIEs follow this distinction as well. The WFOE, EJV and CJV[88] are limited liability companies, while an FICLS is a company limited by shares.

[138] Some FIEs (EJV, CJV) may have their own extensive corporate governance rules that deviate from the *Company Law*, while other FIEs (WFOE, FICLS) generally follow the basic corporate governance regime of the *Company Law*.

86 Exceptions apply, a registered *permanent establishment* of a foreign company being one of them.

87 Articles 3, 22 *2014 Company Registration Regulations*.

88 Note that besides a limited liability company, a CJV can also be set up as a contractual partnership, in which case it is not a legal entity, *see* section 'Cooperative Joint Venture (CJV)' below.

[139] A limited liability company (incl. the WFOE) has either one executive director or a board of directors with three to thirteen members, while a company limited by shares (incl. the FICLS) has a board with five to nineteen members (and for a listed company some of them should be independent directors). The executive director/board, amongst others, carries out shareholders' resolutions regarding business plans, annual budgets, distributions and corporate restructurings (e.g., mergers) and determines the WFOE's internal management structure. The executive director/board should also appoint a general manager (who may be one of the directors) in charge of the day-to-day operations. [89]

[140] The chairman of the board, the executive director (if there is no board) or the general manager should concurrently be appointed as a company's *legal representative*.[90] The legal representative is the only person who has the authority to represent the company externally, except that this person may delegate powers by executing a power of attorney, while documents that have the official company chop affixed to them are also binding on the company (even in the absence of proper internal authorization).

[141] Both a limited liability company and company limited by shares need to appoint a supervisory board with a minimum of three members, except that a limited liability company may also elect to only appoint one or two supervisors. The powers and responsibilities of supervisors are quite limited when compared to supervisory board members in some other countries. Directors and senior officers (including the general manager) may not concurrently serve as a supervisor.[91]

[142] The shareholders' meeting is the highest authority of both a company limited by shares (incl. FICLS) and a limited liability company (incl. WFOE, but excl. EJV/CJV where the board is the highest authority; *see* below).[92] Shareholders exercise voting rights pro rata their capital contributions (different classes of shares with unequal voting rights are in principle not allowed).[93] Resolutions usually require a simple majority, except that the following decisions require a two-thirds majority: amending the company's articles, increase or decrease of the registered capital and the merger, division, dissolution or restructuring of the company.[94] In case of a listed company, a two-thirds majority is also required for any sale of assets or the provision of a guarantee with a value that exceeds 30% of the company's total assets.[95] The *Company Law* does not prescribe mandatory veto rights for investors

[89] Articles 44, 46, 49, 50, 108, 113, 114 *Company Law*.

[90] Article 13 *Company Law*.

[91] Articles 51, 53, 54, 117, 188 *Company Law*.

[92] Articles 36, 98 *Company Law*. If a limited liability company only has one shareholder, there is no shareholders meeting and the sole shareholder simply exercises its powers by written resolutions (Art. 61 *Company Law*). In case of multiple shareholders, written resolutions are allowed if signed by all shareholders (Art. 37 *Company Law*).

[93] The *2014 Preferred Shares Pilot Program* for the first time allows the possibility for listed (and a few unlisted) companies to issue preferred shares. These shares give priority when it comes to distributions but have no voting rights attached to them (with a few exceptions).

[94] Articles 42, 43, 103 *Company Law*.

[95] Articles 98, 103, 121 *Company Law*.

in limited liability companies (as is the case for the EJVs and CJVs; *see* below), but shareholders are allowed to agree on such veto rights in a shareholders' agreement.

[143] In case the holder of equity in a limited liability company wishes to transfer its equity to a third party, the other equity holders have a pre-emptive right to acquire such equity under the same terms and conditions, unless the articles of association provide otherwise.[96]

3.3 Foreign-Invested Enterprises

[144] The Ministry of Commerce (MOFCOM) regularly publishes statistics on foreign direct investment in China, which provide a clear picture of the business vehicles that were popular among foreign investors. The table below shows the number of FIEs incorporated in China since 2012. As mentioned, when the *Foreign Investment Law* becomes effective in January 2020, FIEs will no longer be incorporated.

Number of Foreign-Invested Enterprises (FIE) incorporated in China

FIE Type	*2018*	*2017*	*2016*	*2015*	*2014*	*2013*	*2012*
EJV	10,170	8,364	6,662	5,989	4,824	4,476	4,355
CJV	107	124	126	110	104	142	166
WFOE	50,106	27,007	21,024	20,398	18,809	18,125	20,352
FICLS	129	125	86	78	41	30	52
Total	*60,533*	*35,652*	*27,900*	*26,575*	*23,778*	*22,773*	*24,925*

Source: Website Foreign Investment Department, MOFCOM.

[145] The table above clearly shows that the WFOE is by far the preferred business vehicle among foreign investors. The key reason is that the WFOE is the only FIE in which a foreign investor can have complete control, and no Chinese co-investor is required.

[146] When there is a Chinese co-investor, either because this is required due to foreign investment restrictions or because the foreign investor voluntarily chooses to have a local partner (e.g., to benefit from local expertise or market access), the vehicle of choice is EJV. The main reason that EJV was more popular than CJV is EJV's well-established legal framework.

96 Article 71 *Company Law*.

[147] Before the amendments to the *Company Law* in 2014, the main hurdle for setting up an FICLS was its high minimum registered capital of CNY30m. Even though this requirement has now been abandoned, setting up an FICLS is still quite complicated and is usually only considered for larger enterprises. If there is an intention to IPO, the FICLS is a must, since – as a company limited by shares – it is the only type of FIE that can get its equity listed on a stock exchange.

3.3.1 Wholly Foreign-Owned Enterprise (WFOE)

[148] When investing in an industry that has no limitations on foreign ownership, many foreign investors prefer to incorporate a business vehicle over which they are able to exercise complete control. In such case, foreign investors used to incorporate a WFOE, for which the *WFOE Law* and the *1990 WFOE Implementing Rules* are the key pieces of legislation.[97]

[149] A WFOE is a limited liability company, established by one or more foreign investors (no Chinese investors allowed), with a maximum of fifty.[98] As a limited liability company, a WFOE does not issue shares. Instead, its investors subscribe for an equity interest that corresponds to their relative capital contributions, while the investors' liability is limited to the capital they have agreed to contribute.[99]

[150] In case a WFOE has multiple investors, these investors should file their shareholders' agreement for approval with the PRC authorities, though, in practice, this is often no longer required.[100] In other cases, investors may prefer to incorporate a joint holding vehicle outside of China (Hong Kong being popular) that becomes the sole holder of the WFOE's equity. Their internal shareholders' arrangements are then dealt with at the level of the offshore holding vehicle, which provides more flexibility in terms of (re)structuring, while subsequent equity transfers do not fall under the PRC approval regime.

[151] Since many WFOEs only have one shareholder, corporate governance is usually quite straightforward. Since there are no Chinese investors involved, the WFOE regulations do not provide any special rules on corporate governance either (this in contrast to the EJV/CJV, as discussed hereafter). As a result, the general rules on corporate governance for limited liability companies set forth in the *Company Law* apply (*see* [138] above). There are also no special rules for the powers of shareholders, so the WFOE follows the *Company Law* in this respect as well: the shareholders meeting is the highest authority of a WFOE (contrary to an EJV/CJV) and there are no mandatory veto rights for investors (as is the case for the EJVs and CJVs).

[97] The *1991 WFOE Law Interpretation* further clarifies certain provisions in the *WFOE Law*.

[98] Article 24 *Company Law*. This maximum also applies to limited liability companies that only have domestic investors.

[99] Article 18 *1990 WFOE Implementing Rules*; a WFOE may in theory, upon approval, also take another form than a limited liability company, but in practice this is very rare.

[100] Article 10 *1990 WFOE Implementing Rules*.

[152] The key differences between a WFOE and an ordinary domestic limited liability company, therefore, mainly relate to incorporation procedures (more cumbersome for a WFOE) and capitalization and financing of the company (WFOEs face more restrictions). We will discuss these issues in more detail below (sections 3.4 'Set-Up and Approval of Foreign-Invested Enterprises' – 3.5 'Financing of Foreign-Invested Enterprises').

3.3.2 Equity Joint Venture (EJV)

[153] Due to the restrictions on foreign ownership in a number of industries, some foreign investors have no choice but to invest together with a Chinese joint-venture partner, while in many non-restricted industries, foreign investors voluntarily set up a joint venture to benefit from a Chinese partner's local expertise. Their legal entity of choice used to be the *EJV*, which was created in 1979 as the first business vehicle in China to allow and channel foreign investment. This long-standing history and its widespread use have resulted in a well-established legal framework that provides foreign investors with a reasonable degree of certainty. The *EJV Law* and the *1983 EJV Implementing Rules* are the EJV's key pieces of legislation.

[154] An EJV is a limited liability company,[101] established by at least one Chinese legal entity (i.e., usually not available to Chinese natural persons)[102] and at least one foreign investor (either a legal entity or a natural person). As a limited liability company, an EJV does not issue shares, instead its investors will hold equity interests that correspond to their respective capital contributions. The liability of each investor is limited to its capital contribution.[103]

[155] An important limitation of the EJV is that its profits must be shared in proportion to each investor's capital contribution.[104] There is no possibility to arrange distribution otherwise, so preferred share structures are not an option. The CJV, which we will discuss hereafter, allows for more flexibility in this respect (but the CJV's drawback is that its legal framework is far less developed than that of the EJV).

[156] Foreign investors should, in principle, contribute at least 25% of the registered capital of an EJV.[105] There are some exceptions, but in such event, the business licence (and certain other certificates) will show that the foreign investment percentage is below 25%, resulting in certain benefits (e.g., tax breaks) not being

[101] Article 4 *EJV Law*; Art. 16 *1983 EJV Implementing Rules*.

[102] Article 1 *EJV Law*; Art. 5 *2003 FIE Strengthening Circular*; if a Chinese natural person holds equity in a PRC domestic company and a foreign investor acquires or subscribes for equity in this company (which will then be converted in an EJV), this Chinese natural person may retain such equity upon approval, *see* Art. 5 *2003 FIE Strengthening Circular*; Art. 54 *2006 M&A Rules*; in addition, some districts (e.g., Pudong District in Shanghai) specifically allow an EJV between a foreign party and a Chinese natural person.

[103] Article 16 *1983 EJV Implementing Rules*.

[104] Articles 4, 8 *EJV Law*; Art. 76 *1983 EJV Implementing Rules*.

[105] Article 4 *EJV Law*.

available to the EJV (but in recent years, many of such tax benefits for FIEs have been abolished anyway).[106]

[157] A concept that is often difficult to grasp for foreign investors is that not the equity holders, but the board of the EJV is its highest decision-making body. Each investor has the power to appoint such number of board members as agreed in the joint-venture contract and articles of association.[107] In case of a 50-50 joint venture, the investors usually agree to split their board representatives equally as well. In the event of unequal capital contributions, the majority investor usually also appoints the majority of the board, in which case the minority investor has to rely on contractual veto rights to safeguard its interests.

[158] The following matters require unanimous board approval of all EJV board members attending the meeting: mergers and divisions, termination and dissolution, amendments to the articles of association, and changes in the registered capital.[108] It is not allowed to contractually agree that unanimous approval is not required for these decisions, but it is permitted (and also common) to agree on additional board decisions that require unanimous board approval (thereby balancing the minority investor's inability to block board decisions). The statutory quorum for board meetings is the presence of two-thirds of all directors,[109] but it is allowed (and common) to add the condition that the quorum is only met if each investor is represented by all or at least one of its directors.

[159] A joint-venture partner may only transfer its equity in the EJV upon approval of all other partners.[110] The Supreme Court has decided that this veto right will not be enforced if a partner who refused its approval for the transfer did not purchase the relevant equity by itself (these partners all have a pre-emptive right in accordance with the basic provisions of the *Company Law*, *see* [143]).[111] Local authorities, however, usually still require the signature of all other partners before they are willing to register an equity transfer.

[160] As mentioned, all FIEs need to convert into a regular PRC company within five years after the *Foreign Investment Law* becomes effective in January 2020, which also applies to the EJV. Given the several significant differences described above between a regular limited liability company and the EJV, substantial corporate changes will need to be made to each EJV, while all shareholders need to agree to such changes (probably through their board members). It is not yet clear how this conversion will be implemented, but it is generally expected that complex negotiations between the joint-venture partners could be required in order to timely complete the conversion especially if the relationship between the joint-venture partners is not in a particular good state at that time.

[106] Articles 2–3 *2003 FIE Strengthening Circular*.
[107] Articles 30–31 *EJV Law*.
[108] Articles 32–33 *1983 EJV Implementing Rules*.
[109] Article 32 *1983 EJV Implementing Rules*.
[110] Article 4 *EJV Law*; Arts 2, 9 *1997 FIE Acquisition Rules*.
[111] Article 11 *2010 FIE Disputes Provisions*.

3.3.3 Cooperative Joint Venture (CJV)

[161] Instead of an EJV, foreign investors and their Chinese partners may also choose to set up a Cooperative Joint Venture (CJV). The legal framework for a CJV is much less established than that of the EJV and contains quite a few gaps, resulting in the CJV rarely being used (only 107 CJVs were set up in 2018; *see* [144]). Key regulations are the *CJV Law* and the *1995 CJV Implementing Rules*.

[162] The partners of a CJV should provide the CJV with capital (either in cash or in kind), but they may also contribute 'cooperative means' (not allowed for the EJV), which means the partners provide the CJV with certain assistance – for example, the partners may allow the CJV to use their land, industrial property rights, non-patented technology or other property rights but without actually transferring title of these assets to the CJV.[112] A CJV may take the form of a limited liability company or a contractual partnership, and it has to be established by at least one Chinese legal entity and at least one foreign investor (either a legal entity or a natural person).[113]

[163] In the event of a limited liability company, the CJV does not issue shares – instead, its investors will hold equity interests that correspond to their respective capital contributions, while the liability for each investor is limited to its capital contribution (similar to the EJV). In addition, the investor will be liable for any *cooperative means* it agreed to provide to the CJV.[114] In case of a contractual partnership (which is much less common than the limited liability form), there is no separate legal entity, and each of the investors will have unlimited liability for the CJV's debts.[115]

[164] The key advantage of a CJV is that it offers more flexibility than an EJV when it comes to distributing profits. If the partners agree that the Chinese investor shall receive all residual fixed assets of the CJV for free upon expiry of the CJV's term of operation, the foreign investor may recover its investment ahead of its Chinese partner in the following ways:

(a) obtain a larger share of the profit distributions (compared to the foreign investor's equity stake in the CJV);
(b) recover its investment prior to the CJV paying income tax; or
(c) receive distributions equal to the amount the CJV's fixed assets have depreciated.

These methods are only available if the CJV has settled all of its losses, while methods (b) and (c) also require approval from MOFCOM and the finance and tax

[112] Article 8 *CJV Law*; Art. 18, *1995 CJV Implementing Rules*.
[113] Article 4 *1995 CJV Implementing Rules*; section I, *1996 CJV Implementing Rules Interpretation*.
[114] Article 14 *1995 CJV Implementing Rules*.
[115] Article 50 *1995 CJV Implementing Rules*.

authorities. The foreign investor will be liable for the debts of the CJV up to the aggregate amount of investment recovered ahead of time.[116]

[165] Many other aspects of the CJV are similar to the EJV. The board is also the highest authority, except that if the CJV is a contractual partnership, a so-called *Joint Management Committee* will be its highest authority.[117] Decisions that require unanimous approval are also similar to the EJV, while the quorum for board/joint committee meetings is also two-thirds.[118] The foreign investor in a CJV should also not invest less than 25% of the equity (or if the CJV is not a company, not less than 25% of the total investment contributed by each partner).[119]

3.3.4 Foreign-Invested Company Limited by Shares (FICLS)

[166] Foreign-Invested Company Limited by Shares (FICLS) issues shares to its investors (as opposed to the equity interests issued by a WFOE, EJV and CJV). Before the amendments to the *Company Law* in 2014, the main hurdle for setting up an FICLS was its high minimum registered capital of CNY30m. Even though this requirement has now been abandoned,[120] an FICLS never became very popular among foreign investors given its relatively lengthy and complicated incorporation procedures and the need for a more complex corporate governance structure (e.g., minimum of five board members). A FICLS is, however, the only type of FIE that can be listed on a PRC stock exchange. In practice, most foreign investors, therefore, commence operations through a WFOE or EJV and convert such vehicle into an FICLS by the time of an IPO.

[167] The *1995 FICLS Rules* provide the legal basis for the FICLS, but several restrictions contained therein have been lifted by subsequent regulations.[121] Since these rules only deal with the establishment of an FICLS, or the conversion of another legal entity into an FICLS, many aspects of an FICLS are regulated by the general provisions in the *Company Law* on companies limited by shares.[122]

[168] A FICLS is incorporated by so-called promotors. There should be at least one foreign promotor and one Chinese promotor, while the maximum number of promotors is two hundred. The foreign promotors should jointly subscribe for at least 25% of the shares, and each Chinese promotor should be a company or an organization (no natural persons permitted).[123] The promotors may subscribe for

[116] Article 21 *CJV Law*; Arts 44–45 *1995 CJV Implementing Rules*; Section III *1996 CJV Implementing Rules Interpretation*.

[117] Article 12 *CJV Law*; Art. 24, *1995 CJV Implementing Rules*.

[118] Articles 28–29, *1995 CJV Implementing Rules*.

[119] Article 18 *1995 CJV Implementing Rules*; Section II *1996 CJV Implementing Rules Interpretation*.

[120] Articles 1–2 *2014 FIE Administration Improving Notice*; Art. 1 *2015 FIE Registered Capital Decision*.

[121] For example, the *2014 FICLS Conversion Letter* and the amendments to the *Company Law* in 2014.

[122] Article 25 *1995 FICLS Rules*.

[123] Articles 1, 2, 7 *1995 FICLS Rules*; Art. 78, *PRC Company Law*.

all shares, but they can also IPO immediately as of incorporation. In case of the latter, the promotors need to subscribe for at least 35% of the share capital and at least one promotor should have a three-year profit-making track record.[124]

[169] Instead of incorporating an FICLS as a new company, it is also possible to convert other types of companies into an FICLS. Most foreign investors convert their FIE (WFOE, EJV or CJV) into an FICLS by the time they want their FIE to get listed, in which case the shareholders of the FIE usually act as the FICLS' promotors. The requirement that an FIE should have three years of consecutive profits prior to conversion has been formally relinquished in 2014.[125] Domestic limited liability companies and companies limited by shares (which do not have foreign shareholders) can also be converted into an FICLS. Foreign investors should, in principle, hold at least 25% of the registered capital after conversion, but in practice, foreign shareholding below 25% is permitted, provided the company gives up its status as FIE which may result in it losing certain benefits (*see* [156]).[126]

[170] Promotors are jointly and severally liable for all their capital contributions. In the event the company is ultimately not established, the promotors will also be jointly and severally liable for all liabilities incurred by the FICLS, and they should return all subscription monies received from investors.[127] Promotors are subject to a one-year lock-up period during which they are not permitted to transfer their shares. This lock-up applies from the date of incorporation and then again as of the date of the IPO. Other than that, shares in an FICLS are freely transferable, which is a benefit compared to the EJV, where an equity transfer requires the cooperation of all JV partners (*see* [159]).[128]

[171] The corporate governance and shareholders' rights of an FICLS are similar to those of an ordinary company limited by shares. As already described above, the board of an FICLS consists of five to nineteen members, and its supervisory board should have at least three supervisors. The meeting of shareholders is the highest authority within the company, and each shareholder has one vote for each share it holds. Resolutions require a simple majority, except for a few actions that require a two-thirds majority. It is allowed, and also quite common, to make further arrangements regarding corporate governance in the company's articles. For example, distributions may be made in other proportions than the relative shareholdings (which is not allowed for an EJV) and certain decisions may be made subject to

124 Articles 5, 6 *1995 FICLS Rules*; rt. 84 *PRC Company Law*.

125 Article 15 *1995 FICLS Rules*; *2014 FICLS Conversion Letter*.

126 Articles 2–3 *2003 FIE Strengthening Circular*; *2001 Foreign Investment in Listed Companies Opinions*; these opinions require that the foreign shareholding post-listing is above 10%, but in practice some FICLS with foreign shareholding below 10% also managed to get listed.

127 Articles 93, 94 *Company Law*. Promotors are also jointly and severally liable towards the FICLS in case the company's interests are harmed during its establishment due to the fault of the promotors.

128 Articles 137, 141 *Company Law* (there are also several transfer restrictions for directors, supervisors and senior officers of a company limited by shares). Article 15 *FICLS Rules* still mentions a three-year lock-up, but this no longer applies due to the amended *Company Law*.

shareholder approval (e.g., transfer or acquisition of substantial assets, providing security for third parties).[129]

3.3.5 Foreign-Invested Holding Company (FIHC)

[172] The Foreign-Invested Holding Company (FIHC), also often referred to as a China Holding Company (or CHC), is not a separate type of FIE, since it takes the form of a WFOE (most common), an EJV (less common) or an FICLS (only allowed since October 2015). The key rules governing an FIHC are the *2004 FIHC Provisions*.[130] An FIHC's main feature is that it enables a foreign investor to hold several PRC subsidiaries under one umbrella and centrally manage certain operations for all these subsidiaries. If an FIHC meets certain criteria, it can obtain the status of *Regional Headquarters*, which provides further flexibility and benefits.

[173] Until October 2015, the minimum registered capital of USD30m was a significant hurdle for setting up an FIHC. Although this requirement has now been formally abandoned, in practice some local regulators still require a USD30m capital contribution. Even if the local regulators do not require this, a foreign investor still needs to satisfy several burdensome criteria. The foreign investor needs to demonstrate that it has either: (a) a total asset value of no less than USD400m and established at least one FIE in China to which it has contributed no less than USD10m, or (b) established at least 10 FIEs in China and paid up no less than USD30m in registered capital.[131] Due to these high minimum amounts, the FIHC is in practice only viable for large multinationals. In case an FIHC is set up with a Chinese partner, this Chinese partner needs to have a good credit status and at least CNY100m worth of total assets.

[174] An FIHC is only an investment and services company, and its main limitation is that it is not allowed to directly engage in manufacturing activities. The key advantage of an FIHC is that it may operate as an investment company and invest in any industry open to foreign investors. In addition, an FIHC may provide certain services to its portfolio companies like procurement and sourcing, foreign exchange management, technical support, consulting services, credit support and, upon approval by the China Banking Regulatory Commission (CBRC, financial support. An FIHC may also establish R&D centres within China.[132]

[175] Even though the minimum registered capital requirement has been abandoned, certain additional benefits only become available once USD30m has been contributed as capital and government approval has been obtained. The additional benefits include the right to obtain a higher amount of foreign loans (*see* [209] below), purchase and sell the products manufactured by its portfolio companies,

[129] Articles 104, 166 *Company Law*.

[130] Amended by the *2006 Supplementary FIHC Provisions* and the *2015 FIE Registered Capital Decision*.

[131] Article 3 *2004 FIHC Provisions*; Art. 8 *2015 FIE Registered Capital Decision*.

[132] Articles 10, 13, 28 *2004 FIHC Provisions*.

provide technical training to distributors and lease machines and equipment to portfolio companies (operational lease only).[133]

[176] Obtaining the status of *Regional Headquarters* is more complicated since an FIHC then either requires: (a) a paid-up capital of at least USD100m, or (b) a paid-up capital of USD50m, combined with CNY100m in profits (on a consolidated basis) and the total assets of all enterprises invested in by the FIHC need to be valued at least CNY3bn.[134] Benefits of qualifying as a *Regional Headquarters* include the right to import auxiliary materials, provide logistical services to portfolio companies, establish financing companies (upon CBRC approval) and conduct outsourcing business.[135]

3.4 Set-Up and Approval of Foreign-Invested Enterprises

[177] Below, we set out the various steps that are required when a foreign investor wishes to establish an FIE. Once the *Foreign Investment Law* takes effect in January 2020, foreign investors will no longer be able to establish FIEs, and instead, they will have to incorporate regular limited liability companies and companies limited by shares. The new law does not specify how the set-up and approval process will look like when foreign investors establish these type of entities, but it is expected that the process described for FIEs below will generally apply (although some modifications can be expected in the years to come).

3.4.1 NDRC Approval or Record-Filing

[178] If approval by the National Development and Reform Commission (NDRC) is required, the first step when incorporating an FIE is submitting a project application report to the NDRC. In section 2.4.1 'NDRC Approval or Record-Filin', we set out that NDRC approval is required for the establishment of an FIE if the relevant industry is listed in: (a) the *restricted* category of the *Foreign Investment Catalogue,* or (b) sections 1-10 of the *Domestic Catalogue*. During its approval process, NDRC will carry out a substantive review of the project and the impact on resources, environment, economy and society (*see* further 2.4.1 'NDRC Approval or Record-Filin' for a detailed overview of the NDRC approval process).

[179] If no NDRC approval is required, a foreign investor only needs to submit a simple record-filing to the NDRC when incorporating an FIE ([61]). In practice, however, for many projects, no such record-filing is made, while foreign investors still manage to get all other approvals described below and obtain a business licence for their FIEs (this is mainly true for companies in the service and trading industry and for smaller projects that require relatively little investment).

133 Articles 9, 15 *2004 FIHC Provisions*.

134 Article 22 *2004 FIHC Provisions*.

135 Article 25 *2004 FIHC Provisions*.

3.4.2 Online Preliminary Approval

[180] The next step in the incorporation process in most cities – and the first step for most projects as they are not subject to NDRC approval – is the online filing for preliminary approval with the local AMR.[136] The AMR filing focuses on the details of the company to be established, and it should include the proposed company name, address, business scope, registered capital, corporate governance structure and details of the officers of the proposed company. Upon review, the AMR will provide direct feedback through the online system. The items that the AMR most commonly requires to be amended are the proposed company name and business scope.

[181] In the past, the very first step of a company establishment was name pre-approval: the investor would submit a list of possible names, and depending on availability, one would be reserved. This process is now part of the online preliminary approval by the AMR, but the idea is the same: the AMR will check whether the proposed name meets the relevant criteria and whether it does not conflict with any existing names.

[182] Note that each company in China has a unique Chinese name, and names of FIEs usually consist of: (1) the trade name, (2) the location (city) of the FIE, (3) a reference to the industry, and (4) the organizational form (limited liability company or company limited by shares). The location name can usually be put in front of the name or in between brackets after the trade name of the industry reference. So, for example, it could be *ABC (Shanghai) Trading Company Limited*.

[183] The business scope is a description of the activities that the company *can* engage in. The business scope determines whether special approvals or licences are required (e.g., because it falls within the *Foreign Investment Negative List*, or if the activity is subject to approval from an industry regulator), but local authorities also have their own system and criteria for approving certain business scope language. The key is to ensure that all the company's proposed activities are covered, so as to avoid that later when the business scope needs to be expanded.

3.4.3 MOFCOM Approval or Record-Filing

[184] In section 2.4.2 'MOFCOM Approval or Record-Filing', we discussed that as of October 2016, approval from MOFCOM is no longer required for the establishment of an FIE in an industry outside the *Foreign Investment Negative List*. This means that if the business scope of a new FIE does not contain any business activities covered by the *Foreign Investment Negative List*, only a record-filing with MOFCOM needs to be made – and often this record-filing is made after the *business licence* has been issued though initial information may need to be submitted when filing for online preliminary approval with the AMR. If the business scope does contain activities restricted by the *Foreign Investment Negative List*, incorporation of

[136] *2018 Measures on Filing.*

the FIE still requires MOFCOM approval (except if approval from an industry regulator replaces MOFCOM approval; *see* below).

[185] Although each different type of FIE has its own set of rules that prescribe the basic MOFCOM filing process for which application documents need to be submitted for incorporation,[137] the procedures are nevertheless quite similar for each FIE. In addition, there are several general rules and regulations regarding the MOFCOM approval or record-filing process that apply to all (or most) FIEs.[138]

[186] Whether the application needs to be submitted to central MOFCOM or one of its provincial, municipal or district level departments depends on the location, industry and amount of investment. The higher the level of the authority whose approval is required, the more complicated and time-consuming the process usually will be. Generally speaking, investments that are not listed on the *Foreign Investment Negative List* and have a transaction value of less than USD300m and those projects in *restricted* sectors with a transaction value of less than USD50m can be submitted to a local bureau of MOFCOM, while larger transactions should be approved by central MOFCOM.[139]

[187] The main application documents for obtaining MOFCOM approval, or completing the record-filing, generally include:

(a) an application form setting out the key details of the FIE (e.g., proposed business scope, registered capital);
(b) notarized and legalized incorporation certificates of the FIE's shareholder(s) and passport copies of their authorized representatives;
(c) a list of officers of the FIE (legal representative, board member(s), supervisor(s), general manager);
(d) the proposed joint-venture contract in case of multiple investors (WFOE, EJV, CJV) or the promotor agreement (FICLS);
(e) proof of registered address (lease agreement or title certificate);
(f) certain site-related opinions (if required, e.g., an environmental impact report);
(g) pre-approval from the industry regulator (if required) or documents showing compliance with relevant industry regulations (if MOFCOM needs to consult with the industry regulator); and
(h) a list of goods that will be imported (if applicable).

[188] Note that the above is a general overview only, and specific requirements differ case-by-case depending on the type of FIE and the nature of the investment. An

137 *1990 WFOE Implementing Rules*; *1983 EJV Implementing Rules*; *1995 CJV Implementing Rules*; *1995 FICLS Rules*; *2004 FIHC Provisions*; *2009 FIHC Approval Circular*.

138 *See*, for example: *2016 FIE Filing Measures*; *2010 FIE Approval Delegation Circular*; *2009 Foreign Investment Approval Circular; 2008 Foreign Investment Licensing Circular; 2008 FIE Approval Delegating Circular; 2008 Foreign Investment Handbook*; *2006 FIE Approval Opinions*; *2006 FIE Approval Opinions Interpretations*.

139 *2010 FIE Approval Delegation Circular*; *2009 Foreign Investment Approval Circular*, *2009 FIHC Approval Circular*, *2008 Foreign Investment Licensing Circular*, *2008 FIE Approval Delegating Circular*.

applicant should also at all times consult with the relevant department of MOFCOM prior to filing since each local MOFCOM department has wide discretion (which is regularly exercised) to demand additional documents or require that documents are in a certain form.[140] MOFCOM regularly rejects applications if it deems these are incomplete or not in the required form, although it is usually acceptable to cure such defects and resubmit an application later. However, in case of an online record-filing, an applicant will only be granted a one-time fifteen business-day period to supplement an incomplete application, *see* [193] below.

[189] In case MOFCOM *approval* is required (for *record-filings see* [193] below), the MOFCOM officials will scrutinize the application documents, and they may reject an application if the establishment of the FIE:

(a) may damage China's sovereignty or social and public interest;
(b) could endanger China's national security;
(c) violates any PRC laws and regulations;
(d) is inconsistent with the requirements of China's national economic development;
(e) would pollute the environment; or
(f) impairs the rights and interest of one party due to obvious unfairness in the contracts and articles of association (applies only to joint ventures).[141]

In practice, the key evaluation criteria is whether the application and establishment comply with all relevant PRC laws and regulations, and rejections on the basis of any of the other criteria are quite uncommon.

[190] As mentioned ([136]), companies in China are not allowed to carry out revenue-generating activities outside their business scope, so MOFCOM will carefully review each proposed business scope and check whether the activities are:

(a) prohibited in the *Foreign Investment Negative List*;
(b) *restricted* by the *Foreign Investment Negative List*, and if so, whether the relevant restrictions have been complied with (e.g., limits on foreign shareholding); and
(c) subject to industry-specific regulations, and if so, whether these have been complied with (this is either confirmed by pre-approval of the relevant industry regulator or by MOFCOM consulting with such regulator, *see* [76]).

[191] MOFCOM may also still scrutinize the articles of association and the joint-venture contract (in case of multiple investors) and may require investors to make certain changes to these documents because it deems them incompliant with PRC law or with MOFCOM's internal policies and requirements. These internal policies

140 Article 10 *1990 WFOE Implementing Rules*: Art. 7 *1983 EJV Implementing Rules*; Art. 7 *CJV Implementing Rules*; Art. 9 *1995 FICLS Rules*; Art. 6 *2004 FIHC Rules*.

141 Article 5 *1990 WFOE Implementing Rules*, Art. 4 *1983 EJV Implementing Rules* (does not explicitly mention ground b)); Art. *9 CJV Implementing Rules* (does not explicitly mention ground d)). Note that the *1995 FICLS Rules* do not explicitly mention any of these rejection criteria.

and requirements vary from location to location, and especially in more remote areas, officials are known to reject complex provisions in joint-venture contracts due to their lack of experience therewith.

[192] MOFCOM has ninety days to decide on the approval of a WFOE and EJV, while it has forty-five days for a CJV and FICLS.[142] Note that this time frame only applies as of the moment MOFCOM deems an application complete, while it has wide discretion to demand additional information or changes to the application documents. In practice, however, MOFCOM approval can usually be obtained within twenty business days of a complete application, unless MOFCOM needs to consult with an industry regulator (*see* below).

[193] In case only a *record-filing* with MOFCOM is required (i.e., the relevant industry is not on the *Foreign Investment Negative List*), the filing can be submitted online with the competent MOFCOM bureau. MOFCOM will check if the filing is complete and accurate, and whether the establishment of the FIE indeed only requires a record-filing. If there are no issues, MOFCOM will accept the record-filing online within three business days, and the applicant may collect a record-filing receipt thereafter. If the incorporation of the FIE falls outside the scope of the record-filing framework (e.g., the relevant industry is on the *Foreign Investment Negative List*), the filing will be rejected. If the filing is deemed incomplete or inaccurate, the applicant will be granted a one-time fifteen--business day period to supplement the application.[143]

3.4.4 Industry Regulator Approval

[194] In section 2.3 'Industry-Specific Restrictions', we discussed that more a hundred business activities require additional, industry-specific licensing, which may come with additional qualification criteria (e.g., minimum amount of assets owned by the foreign investor, minimum amount of registered capital of the FIE, or track record in the relevant industry). When incorporating an FIE that has a business scope that includes any of these regulated activities, approval from the relevant industry regulator is usually required. This approval process mainly involves a check on whether all the qualification criteria for the licensed business scope have been met.

[195] As discussed above ([76]), industry regulator approval is usually connected to the general MOFCOM investment approval or record-filing in one of the following ways:

(a) pre-approval from the industry regulator is required before submitting the investment to MOFCOM for approval (e.g., medical institutions, telecom);

---

[142] Article 11 *WFOE Implementing Rules*, Art. 8 *EJV Implementing Rules*, Art. 7 *CJV Implementing Rules*; Art. 9 *FICLS Provisions*.

[143] Articles 7, 11, 12 *2016 FIE Filing Measures*.

(b) MOFCOM seeks the opinion of the industry regulator (which can also be other departments of MOFCOM) during its own approval process (e.g., construction engineering services, distribution, retail, leasing and international freight forwarding);
(c) industry regulator directly approves the foreign investment and no general approval by MOFCOM is required (e.g., banks, foreign legal services); or
(d) post-approval from the industry regulator is required after MOFCOM approval or record-filing (and usually also after obtaining the business licence; e.g., the food industry).

3.4.5 Business Licence and Post-approval Registrations

[196] The incorporation should be completed with SAMR or, more commonly, with a local AMR at provincial, municipal or district level. The competent AMR will issue the FIE its business licence, which marks the formal establishment of the company.

[197] We note that in case only a record-filing with MOFCOM is required, both the *2016 FIE Filing Measures* (issued by MOFCOM) and the *2016 FIE Filing Circular* (issued by SAMR) allow for the possibility to obtain a business licence with the AMR first and complete the record-filing with MOFCOM within thirty days thereafter.[144] In practice and for historical reasons, however, some local AMRs still require the record-filing receipt issued by MOFCOM to be submitted to them before they are willing to issue the business licence.

[198] Usually, obtaining a business licence from AMR is a formality that does not involve a substantive review of the application documents. However, AMRs are known to require amendments to a company's proposed business scope, for example, because local officials hold the view that the activities under the proposed business scope are subject to a licence (and such licence should be obtained prior to the issuance of the business licence), or sometimes simply because the officials are unfamiliar with the proposed wording of a business scope (in which case, they require the scope to be reworded into something more mainstream).

[199] Since October 2015, the business licence issued by AMR also includes the newly established company's organization code certificate and tax registration certificate. As of October 2016, the social insurance registration and statistics certificate are also included in the business licence. Previously, these certificates had to be obtained separately, which was burdensome and time-consuming, so this is definitely a positive development for foreign investors.[145]

[200] After issuance of the business licence, the newly established FIE needs to go through a series of time-consuming post-formation registrations with various authorities and the bank (e.g., foreign exchange, bank account opening permit,

[144] Article 11 *2016 FIE Filing Measures*; Art. 3 *2016 FIE Filing Circular*.

[145] Article 1 *2015 Registration Reform Opinions*; *2016 Business License Reform Notice*.

customs, VAT registration) before it can be fully operational. Most of these steps are mere formalities and do not entail any substantive review process.

3.5 Financing of Foreign-Invested Enterprises

3.5.1 Registered and Paid-up Capital

[201] Since the latest amendments to the *Company Law* in 2014, there are no longer minimum registered capital requirements for limited liability companies and companies limited by shares. This means that investors may decide for themselves how much registered capital they wish to contribute, and also at which point in time they will make their contributions (payment in instalments after incorporation is, therefore, also allowed). Investors do need to set out the timing of their contributions in the articles of association, and they are liable towards both the company and their fellow shareholders to timely make the contributions to which they have committed themselves.[146]

[202] This flexibility does not only apply to PRC companies that only have domestic investors but also to FIEs.[147] Some FIEs (e.g., telecom industry ([51]), Regional Headquarters (section 3.3.5 'Foreign-Invested Holding Company (FIHC)')) are, however, still subject to minimum capital requirements, although in many industries these requirements for foreign investors were lifted in 2015.[148]

[203] Even though most minimum registered capital requirements have been abandoned, foreign investors should still try to ensure that their company is sufficiently capitalized from incorporation since these funds will become the company's initial working capital. Although it is possible to subsequently increase a company's registered capital, the approval and registration procedures that must be completed take a considerable amount of time (several weeks) and result in administrative costs. However, the registered capital should also not be set too high, since lowering it at a later stage can be extremely burdensome, and in practice, local authorities may simply reject it (although, in some cities, the attitude of local governments towards capital decreases has improved over the past few years).

[204] While there are alternative means of financing, these have drawbacks. A subsidiary may only take out a foreign bank loan or a shareholder loan in accordance with the approved foreign debt quota (*see* section 3.5.2 'Financing with Foreign Loans' below), and this process takes time. Financing through related-party transactions is also common, especially in emergencies, but this results in fiscal inefficiencies as payments for trade and services are taxable in China. In many cases, it

---

146 Articles 28, 80, 83, 93 *Company Law*. Note that for companies limited by shares (incl. FICLS) this only applies to the promotors, who are also jointly liable for each other's contributions (*see* [170]).

147 Articles 1–2 *2014 FIE Administration Improving Notice*. In addition, the *2014 Registered Capital Decision* explicitly confirmed some of these changes for the WFOE, EJV and CJV, while the *2015 FIE Registered Capital Decision* did so for the FICLS and FIHC.

148 *2015 FIE Registered Capital Decision*.

is, therefore, advisable to set the registered capital at such level that the company is able to finance its operations until it is generating some meaningful cash flow.

[205] Capital contributions are usually made in foreign currency, but onshore CNY income may also be reinvested (e.g., dividends received in CNY), while CNY that has been lawfully obtained offshore may be used for capital contributions as well.[149] The mandatory verification of registered capital contributions by a public certified accountant as a condition for conversion into CNY has been abolished in 2014,[150] but in practice, some banks or local authorities still require FIEs to engage a *CPA* firm to verify the capital contribution.

[206] FIEs need to open a special capital account with their bank in order to be able to receive capital contributions. Previously, FIEs were required to register with SAFE before they could open such capital account, but since June 2015, SAFE has delegated this, so the registration can be done directly with designated banks. In June 2015, it also became possible to convert capital contributions paid in foreign currency into CNY at will (previously, FIEs had to provide supporting documents to prove the lawful use of these funds before they were allowed to convert capital contributions into CNY).[151]

[207] The subsequent outward transfer from the capital account of capital contributions is, however, still subject to restrictions. These capital contributions may only be applied for carrying out activities within the FIE's business scope, while certain specific transactions are prohibited (e.g., no investment in securities, no purchase of real estate not for self-use and no disbursement of loans to non-affiliated parties). When applying to the bank to transfer out registered capital that has been converted into CNY, supporting documents to prove the authenticity of the transaction are still required (e.g., contracts, invoices, customs documents). Besides authenticity, the bank also needs to verify that outward transfers of registered capital are within the FIE's business scope and comply with said restrictions.[152]

[208] Registered capital may also be contributed in kind, unless the law provides otherwise (e.g., the FIHC, where the contribution needs to be all cash[153]). In-kind contributions need to be valued by a qualified appraisal company and may not be over- or under-valued.[154] Prior to the 2014 *Company Law* amendments, at least 30% of the registered capital had to be contributed in cash, but this rule has now been abandoned, making a 100% non-cash contribution possible. A wide variety of assets may be contributed as registered capital, including property rights, land-use

149 Article 25 *1990 WFOE Implementing Rules*, Art. 2 *2012 Forex FDI Circular*; Art. 1 *2013 RMB Direct Investment Announcement*.

150 Article 1 *2014 FIE Administration Improving Notice*.

151 *2015 Forex FDI Circular*; *2015 Forex Reform Circular*.

152 Articles 2, 4, 5 *2016 Capital Account Reform Circular* (exceptions apply to the restrictions mentioned); *2015 Forex Reform Circular*. Note that for smaller amounts some banks allow the outward transfer of registered capital under the condition that the required evidence proving authenticity is provided afterwards.

153 Article 7 *2004 FIHC Rules*.

154 Articles 27, 83, 93 *Company Law*, *see also* the *2009 Non-cash Contributions Notice*. This requirement is not set out explicitly for companies limited by shares (incl. FICLS).

rights, technology, intellectual property rights and even equity in other PRC companies (restrictions apply). Labour, the ability to obtain credit, the name of a natural person, goodwill, franchising rights and encumbered assets may, however, not be contributed as registered capital.[155]

3.5.2 Financing with Foreign Loans

[209] FIEs may only borrow foreign debt up to a strict quota, which includes loans from both the foreign parent company and foreign lending institutions.[156] An important concept in this respect is the FIE's *total investment* that each FIE has to specify in its articles of association. The *total investment* is the sum of an FIE's: (a) *registered capital*, and (b) its *headroom* to obtain foreign debt financing. In other words, the difference between an FIE's *total investment* and its *registered capital* is the maximum amount for which an FIE may obtain financing through foreign loans. Note that foreign debt with a tenor of one year or longer consumes the borrowing headroom permanently, meaning that even if such loan is repaid by the FIE, the FIE is not permitted to use that headroom again.[157]

[210] The maximum total investment of an FIE is determined by the amount of its registered capital – the higher the registered capital, the higher the FIE may set its total investment. The table below sets out the details of the applicable ratios:

Total Investment (USD)	*Minimum Registered Capital (USD)*
Ordinary FIEs (WFOE, EJV, CJV)	
Up to 3m (inclusive)	7/10 of the Total Investment
Between 3m and 10m (inclusive)	The higher of: 2.1m and 1/2 of the Total Investment
Between 10m and 30m (inclusive)	The higher of: 5m and 2/5 of the Total Investment
More than 30m	The higher of: 12m and 1/3 of the Total Investment

[155] Articles 6–7 *2014 Registered Capital Provisions*. *See* the *2012 FIE Equity Contribution Provisions* (amended by the *2015 FIE Registered Capital Decision*) for contributing equity in another PRC company as registered capital of an FIE.

[156] Technically speaking the same restrictions apply to domestic borrowings, but in practice only foreign currency borrowings from entities outside the PRC are restricted.

[157] Key rules are to be found in the *1987 FIE Registered Capital Regulations;* Art. 9 2004 *FIHC Provisions*; *2003 Foreign Debt Management Measures*, *2013 Foreign Debt Registration Guidelines*. Note that in some cities local SAFE no longer applies the rule that headroom is permanently consumed in case of long-term loans.

Total Investment (USD)	*Minimum Registered Capital (USD)*
Foreign-Invested Holding Companies	
Between 150m and 500m	1/5 of the Total Investment
As of 500m	1/7 of the Total Investment

[211] A few examples to clarify the above:

(a) if an FIE has a registered capital of USD1m, its total investment may be as high as USD 1 428 571 (= USD1m / 0.7), in which case it can obtain foreign debt up to USD 428 571 (= total investment minus registered capital);
(b) with a registered capital of USD1.8m, the total investment is maximum USD2 571 429 (= USD1.8m / 0.7), and the borrowing headroom is USD772 429 (the next bracket of USD3-10m total investment is not yet available, since the minimum registered capital of USD 2.1 has not been met); and
(c) with a registered capital of USD3m, the total investment is a maximum of USD6m (= USD3m / 0.5), so the borrowing headroom is USD3m as well.

[212] In January 2017, People's Bank of China (PBOC) issued the *2017 Foreign Debt Notice*, which introduced a new system to determine the foreign debt quota. FIEs were granted a one-year transitional period (i.e., until January 2018) in which they may elect to continue using the old system described above. Although the rules state that a further assessment by PBOC and SAFE will need to take place when the transitional period expires[158], so far, no assessment results have been published. In practice, both the old and new system seem to apply alongside each other. Once the *Foreign Investment Law* enters into effect in January 2020 and foreign investors will have to set up regular PRC companies, it is expected that for such new companies, only the new system of foreign debt will be available.

[213] Under the old system, the amount of registered capital determines the borrowing headroom. Under the new rules, the key factor in determining the maximum amount of foreign debt is the company's *net asset value* (or *capital* in case of a financial institution). Non-financial institutions may borrow foreign debt up to 200% of the amount of their net assets, provided that: (a) PBOC may adjust this percentage on the basis of macroeconomic considerations (macro-prudential ratio) and their risk policy (financing leverage ratio), and (b) the outstanding amount of debt will be adjusted on the basis of a risk weighting that depends on the type of foreign debt.[159]

[214] In 2016, both the macro-prudential ratio and the financing leverage ratio were initially set at one (i.e., 100%), but in 2017, the financing leverage ratio was

158 Article 13 *2017 Foreign Debt Notice*.
159 Article 3 *2017 Foreign Debt Notice*.

increased to two (i.e. 200%), meaning that corporates could attract twice as much foreign debts.[160]

[215] The risk weighting of foreign debt means that loans (except foreign trade finance) with a tenor of longer than one year are included in the calculation for their full amount, while loans with a shorter tenor count for 150%. If the debt is in foreign currency, 50% of the loan amount has to be added to the initial calculation. A foreign currency loan with a tenor of one year or shorter, therefore, counts for 200% (=150%+50%).[161]

[216] The table below summ*arizes* the calculation method for non-financial institutions:

Risk-weighted limit	*Type of foreign debt*	*Risk ratio*
Net Asset Value x 2 (financing leverage ratio) x 1 (macro-prudential ratio)	CNY/foreign currency debt > 1-year tenor (excl. trade finance)	**1**
	+	
	CNY/foreign currency debt ≤ 1-year tenor (excl. trade finance)	**1.5**
	+	
	All foreign currency debt (excl. trade finance)	**0.5**

[217] Foreign trade credit and foreign trade financing are not considered foreign debt and do not consume the borrowing headroom. The same applies to participation in a regulated cross-border cash pooling scheme and the capitalization of debt.[162]

[218] Whether FIEs should already move to the new regime or stick to the old rules depends on their specific situation. An advantage of the new system is that loans with a tenor of one year or longer do not permanently consume the borrowing headroom (as opposed to the old system, [209]). If an FIE has a high registered capital but a low net asset value, it may, however, be beneficial to stick to the current system, since the quota may be lower under the new rules.

[219] Loans obtained by FIEs from outside China (including shareholder loans) require registration with SAFE (under the new rules corporate borrowers should do

160 Article 6 *2017 Foreign Debt Notice*.

161 Articles 5, 9 *2017 Foreign Debt Notice*.

162 Article 4 *2017 Foreign Debt Notice*. Note that only the most important exceptions are listed here, several other forms of foreign debt are also excluded from the calculation.

so at least three business days prior to drawdown), and the corresponding cross-border loan agreements only take effect upon completion of such registration.[163] In September 2016, it became possible for FIEs to convert foreign currency received as a foreign loan into CNY at will (previously, FIEs had to provide supporting documents to prove the lawful use of these funds before they were allowed to convert loans into CNY).[164]

[220] The subsequent outward transfer of these converted loans is, however, subject to the same restrictions as mentioned above for capital contributions. These loans may, therefore, only be applied for carrying out activities within the FIE's business scope, while certain specific transactions are prohibited (e.g., no investment in securities, no purchase of real estate not for self-use and no disbursement of loans to non-affiliated parties). In addition, short-term loans are mainly to be used as working capital and not for medium- or long-term purposes, such as investments in fixed assets. When applying to the bank to transfer out a loan that has been converted into CNY, supporting documents to prove the authenticity of the transaction are still required (e.g., contracts, invoices, customs documents), and the bank needs to verify that such outward transfers are within the FIE's business scope and comply with said restrictions.[165]

3.6 Other Business Vehicles Available to Foreign Investors

3.6.1 Representative Office (RO)

[221] While the FIE (or as of 2020 when the *Foreign Investment Law* becomes effective, the limited liability company or a company limited by shares) is the most important vehicle for a foreign investor to expand into China, there are alternatives. To a foreign company that wants a presence in China without the financial commitment that goes with establishing an FIE, there is another option. An Representative Office (RO) allows a foreign company to have an office in China, hire employees (albeit indirectly through an employment agent if it concerns Chinese employees), open bank accounts and pay for expenses. The advantage of an representative office is that it does not require an initial capital investment, since the foreign parent company will only need to remit capital to the bank account of the representative office from time to time, to ensure that the representative office is able to pay its expenses. Another advantage of the representative office is that establishment procedures are comparatively simple, as such establishment is not

163 Article 10 *2017 Foreign Debt Notice*; Art. 22 *2003 Foreign Debt Management Measures; 2013 Foreign Debt Registration Guidelines*; *2013 Foreign Debt Administrative Measures*. In case of foreign debt that has a tenor of more than 12 months, registration with NDRC may also be required, *see 2015 NDRC Foreign Debt Circular*.

164 Articles 1, 2 *2016 Capital Account Reform Circular*.

165 Articles 2, 4, 5 *2016 Capital Account Reform Circular* (exceptions apply to the restrictions mentioned); Art. 27 *2003 Foreign Debt Management Measures*.

subject to MOFCOM approval or record-filing and only requires registration with the AMR.[166]

[222] The greatest limitation to having an representative office is that under the *1980 Rep Office Regulations* and the 2011 RO Registration Regulations, an representative office is only permitted to engage in non-direct-profit-making operations, such as liaison, research and marketing. This means that the RO is strictly prohibited from signing contracts on behalf of the parent company, collecting money, issuing invoices to domestic companies or individuals, representing a third party other than its own parent company in the business or carrying out any other business operations. If an RO ignores the forgoing restrictions and engages in any profit-making activities, the AMR may forfeit the profit, impose a penalty up to CNY500 000 and even revoke the RO's registration certificate.[167]

[223] A second drawback to the representative office is that it is not an independent legal person in China. Therefore, both during its operations and after its liquidation, the parent company remains liable for all outstanding liabilities. An RO cannot be transferred to a third party (whether domestic or foreign) nor can it be converted into an FIE. Where it no longer serves the parent company's purpose, the only way to exit an representative office is to have it liquidated and de-registered (which is a lengthy and cumbersome process).[168]

[224] The *2011 RO Registration Regulations* impose a significant restriction on a foreign enterprise that desires to establish an representative office in China since it requires such foreign enterprise to have been in existence for at least two years. The AMR requires evidence in this respect, such as a lease agreement and incorporation documents of the foreign enterprise, which usually should be provided every year.[169]

[225] A final challenge to holding an representative office is fiscal. Although an RO may not earn any income, it is still taxed in China, usually on the basis of its total cost. To calculate corporate income tax, the PRC tax authorities used to work with a deemed profit rate of 10% over RO's total costs, but in 2010, this has been increased to at least 15%.[170] Together with the cancellation of tax exemption policies, this has made representative offices much more expensive to operate. During the past few years, many investors have, therefore, replaced their representative offices with a simple WFOE. These WFOEs provide China-based services to their foreign investors, for which the foreign parent company pays a service fee that is equal to the running costs of the WFOE and usually a deemed profit rate of 5%-15% of the service fee.

166 Article 5 *2011 RO Registration Regulations*; some exceptions apply, ROs of foreign banks are, for example, approved by the CBRC.

167 Articles 13–14, 35 *2011 RO Registration Regulations.*

168 Article 16 *1980 Rep Office Regulations.*

169 Article 23(2) *2011 RO Registration Regulations.*

170 *2010 Rep Office Tax Collection Interim Measures.*

3.6.2 Foreign Invested Partnership (FIP)

[226] In November 2009, the State Council promulgated the *2009 FIP Measures*, which came into effect on 1 March 2010, soon followed by the *2010 FIP Registration Provisions* (also effective 1 March 2010), while minor revisions following in March 2014 and August 2019. In these Measures and Provisions, SAMR provides more detailed regulations.

[227] Under these regulations, a foreign company or individual is allowed to establish an Foreign-Invested Partnership (FIP) with other foreign partners or with Chinese partners (including Chinese companies, individuals and other organizations). The *Partnership Law*, which applies to domestic partnerships, also applies to an FIP, unless the *FIP Measures* or *2010 FIP Registration Provisions* provide otherwise.[171]

[228] There are three forms of FIPs:[172]

(1) *General partnerships* are formed by general partners only. The general partners bear unlimited joint and several liabilities for the debts of the partnership.
(2) *Limited liability partnerships* are formed by one or more general partners and one or more limited partners (having only limited partners is not allowed). The general partners bear unlimited joint and several liabilities for the debts of the partnership, while limited partners bear liability for the partnership's debts to the extent of their individual capital contributions.
(3) *Special general partnerships* are only available to professional services organizations such as law firms and accounting firms. A partner bears unlimited liability, alone or jointly and severally, for liabilities incurred by the partnership due to his (their) intentional act or gross negligence, while the other partner(s) bear liability for the debts to the extent of their capital contributions. All partners bear joint and several liabilities for the debts not incurred due to any partner's intentional act or gross negligence and other debts of the partnership enterprise.

[229] FIPs are subject to the restrictions on foreign investment set forth in the *Foreign Investment Catalogue* (*see* section 2.1.1 'The Foreign Investment Negative List'), which means that foreign investors are not allowed to enter into an FIP if the investment project falls into the *prohibited* category. If a project falls into the *restricted* or *encouraged* category *and* foreign shareholding is limited, an FIP is not permitted to carry out these activities. In case the proposed business scope of the FIP requires any approval from an industry regulator (*see* section 2.4.4 'Industry Regulator Approvals'), such approval shall be obtained prior to the establishment of the FIP.[173]

[171] Articles 2–3 *2009 FIP Measures*; Arts 2–3 *2010 FIP Registration Provisions*.
[172] Article 11 *2010 FIP Registration Provisions*; Arts 2, 55, 57, 75 *Partnership Law*.
[173] Articles 3, 13 *2009 FIP Measures*; Art. 3 *2010 FIP Registration Provisions*.

[230] An FIP is established directly upon completion of registration with the competent AMR, which means that it (unlike FIEs) does not require general investment approval from, or record-filing with, MOFCOM. There is no requirement for any minimum capital contribution, and the foreign partner can make its capital contribution in cash (including foreign currency and local currency legally obtained in China) or in kind, such as intellectual property, land-use rights or other properties. The law even expressly allows a foreign general partner to contribute to the partnership in the form of labour services (which is not allowed for FIEs).[174]

[231] Benefits compared to the EJV are that FIPs are not required to distribute profit in accordance with each partner's capital contribution; partnership interests can be transferred without consent of the other partners (provided the partners agreed thereto in their partnership agreement); and partners have quite some freedom to structure the corporate governance of the partnership as they deem fit.[175]

3.6.3 Domestic Subsidiaries of Foreign-Invested Enterprises

[232] An FIE is permitted to establish a regular domestic *limited liability company* or *company limited by shares*. Such domestic subsidiary is not considered an FIE, but its business licence will state that its shareholder is an FIE. The regular limitations of the *Foreign Investment Negative List* apply as well, which means that an FIE may not hold any equity in a domestic-owned company that is active in any *prohibited* industry, while the FIE needs to comply with all relevant regulations of *restricted* industries (e.g., limitations on foreign ownership).[176]

[233] If an FIE establishes a domestic subsidiary in an industry that is not on the *Foreign Investment Negative List*, the FIE only needs to make a record-filing with the AMR, and no MOFCOM approval or record-filing is required. When an FIE intends to establish a domestic subsidiary that will operate in a *restricted* industry, MOFCOM's approval is, however, required.[177]

[234] Previously, FIEs faced several restrictions when incorporating domestic subsidiaries, but many of those restrictions have been lifted in recent years. For example, FIEs were not permitted to use their own registered capital to contribute capital to such subsidiaries, FIEs could invest no more than 50% of their net asset value in these subsidiaries, and FIEs were only allowed to set up a subsidiary after their registered capital had been fully paid-up and they had started to make profits – these restrictions have all been removed (though subject to certain conditions, for example, using registered capital as capital contribution to subsidiaries are applicable only to FIEs with investment as the primary business, and a special bank account shall be applied and opened for such contribution).[178] Until recently, since registered capital can only be used for activities within the approved or registered

[174] Article 5 *2009 FIP Measures*; Art. 5, 12, 14, 15 *2010 FIP Registration Provisions*.

[175] Articles 18, 26–31, 33, 69, 73 *Partnership Law*.

[176] Articles 3, 4 *2000 FIE Investment Provisions*.

[177] Articles 7–10 *2000 FIE Investment Provisions*.

[178] Article 7 *2006 FIE Approval Opinions*, Art. 5 *2006 FIE Approval Opinions Interpretations*, Art. 2 *2015 FIE Registered Capital Decision* and Art. 4 *2015 Forex Reform Circular*.

business scope, Chinese banks (acting on behalf of the SAFE to supervise the use of foreign currency) have continued to disallow FIE's to settle and use registered capital for investment purposes. Hopefully, this practice will soon give way now that the SAFE has weighed in on the subject.[179]

4 MERGERS & ACQUISITIONS

4.1 Introduction

[235] In this section 'Mergers & Acquisitions', we will focus on private M&A transactions in China (public M&A is outside the scope of this publication). We will first describe the Chinese regulatory framework for each of the most common types of private M&A transactions: equity acquisitions (section 4.2 'Equity Acquisitions'), subscriptions for new equity (section 4.3 'Subscription For New Equity'), asset acquisitions (section 4.4 'Share Swaps'), share swaps (section 4.5 'Asset Acquisitions'), mergers (section 4.6 'Mergers') and the acquisition of state-owned assets (section 4.7 'Acquisition of State-Owned Assets'). At the end of this section 'Mergers & Acquisitions', we will set out which government approval or record-filing procedures are usually required for private M&A transactions in China (section 4.8 'Government Approval For M&A Transactions').

4.2 Equity Acquisitions

4.2.1 Acquiring an Entire PRC Domestic-Owned Company

[236] The most common M&A transaction that involves foreign investment is the one where a foreign investor acquires the entire equity of a domestic-owned enterprise (i.e., a company that only has domestic shareholders). This structure is attractive primarily because it brings into the fold a comprehensive, fully operational business with all the assets and licences that are necessary to continue operating the business with no delay. The target company is bought as is and includes employees, existing vendor and customer relationships and established government relations. The *2006 M&A Rules* are the key piece of legislation for this type of transaction. It is expected that these *2006 M&A Rules* will continue to apply for at least some time after the *Foreign Investment Law* comes into force in January 2020.

[237] While most of the terms and conditions to this type of transaction may be freely agreed upon between the parties, the *2006 M&A Rules* do provide some legal restrictions. As these may influence the transaction, parties should take them into account when negotiating the deal.

[179] Articles 2,4, *2019 SAFE Notice on Cross-border Trade and Investment.*

[238] First of all, each transaction requires approval from Ministry of Commerce (MOFCOM), which is not a mere formality. Approval authorities have broad discretion in requesting changes to the application, documentation and even to the commercial terms, and they will frequently use their authority, which may considerably prolong the process. This makes it important to involve these authorities at an early stage of the transaction to ensure a smooth approval process (see further 4.8 'Government Approval for M&A Transactions' below).[180] If the foreign investor is controlled by a PRC company or national, the acquisition (a so-called *round-trip investment*) requires additional approval (which is in practice seldom granted).[181]

[239] Upon completion of the transaction, the domestic target company shall, until 1 January 2020, convert into a Wholly Foreign-Owned Enterprise (WFOE) (*see* section 3.3.1 'Wholly Foreign-Owned Enterprise (WFOE)'). When the *Foreign Investment Law* comes into force in January 2020, such conversion shall no longer occur, but the transaction shall still be subject to the *Foreign Investment Negative List* (*see* section 2.1.1 'The Foreign Investment Negative List'). This means that the acquisition of an entire domestic-owned company by a foreign investor is not permitted for any *prohibited* industry, while the same is true for most *restricted* industries, since those often require a Chinese joint-venture partner (in which case the acquisition of the *entire* company is not permitted, but a *partial* acquisition (*see* section 4.2.2 'Acquiring Part of a PRC Domestic-Owned Company' below) may be possible).

[240] If the target operates in a regulated industry, approval by the industry regulator is usually required, and if certain qualification criteria apply with respect to the (foreign) shareholder (*see* [47]), the foreign investor shall need to establish that it meets those criteria. All restrictions on capitalization and foreign debt as discussed above in section 3.5 'Financing of Foreign-Invested Enterprises' shall apply to the target as soon as the transaction has been completed.[182]

[241] It is mandatory that the equity purchase agreement between the buyer and seller is governed by PRC law,[183] and this agreement should of course also comply with the *2006 M&A Rules* and other relevant PRC regulations. We will, therefore, set out the key requirements below. As mentioned above, the approval authorities will scrutinize this agreement, and they have the power to request changes thereto.

[242] The transaction price should be determined on the basis of the value of the equity that will transfer as valued by a qualified asset appraisal institution. It is not allowed to sell equity below such valuated price.[184] This appraisal report is one of the documents to be submitted to the approval authorities; although in practice, authorities have adopted different requirements on exactly how the appraised

[180] Article 6 *2006 M&A Rules*, except in a few industries approval from the industry regulator is required instead of MOFCOM approval, *see* [339].

[181] Article 11 *2006 M&A Rules*; the *2008 Foreign Investment Handbook* sets forth some limited circumstances under which MOFCOM may consider granting approval for a round-trip investment.

[182] Articles 4, 9, 19 *2006 M&A Rules*.

[183] Article 22 *2006 M&A Rules*.

[184] Article 14 *2006 M&A Rules*.

value should relate to the transaction price. Another, and often more important, function of the valuation is that the appraised value may be referred to by the tax authorities when they determine whether the seller has obtained any capital gains from its investment and, therefore, whether income taxes should be imposed on this capital gain. It is not uncommon for authorities to suspect that part of the transaction price is paid offshore and, therefore, out of their sight. They will, therefore, often prefer to ignore the transaction price, and instead determine the amount of taxes that are due on the basis of the appraisal report.[185]

[243] The *2006 M&A Rules* also set time restrictions on the payment of the transaction price. A foreign investor acquiring equity in a domestic-owned company must within three months from the date of issuance of the renewed business licence pay the transaction price to the seller. If circumstances exist that make it necessary to extend this time limit, the foreign investor shall, with agreement of the seller and upon approval of the competent authority, pay at least 60% of the purchase price within six months from the date of issuance of the renewed business licence and pay the remaining balance within one year. If any dividends are declared during this period, these need to be paid in proportion to the part of the transaction price that the foreign investor has actually paid.[186] These rules are designed to protect domestic companies against foreign investors with sufficient bargaining power to dictate their own terms. It does, however, make it difficult to implement some mechanisms that are commonly used to protect buyers (e.g., earn-outs and escrow arrangements).

[244] Due to foreign exchange controls, payment of the purchase price can only be made by the purchaser itself (i.e., payments by third parties are not permitted) into a special bank account opened by the Chinese seller for the sole purpose of receiving the purchase price. Approval by SAFE used to be required before such account could be opened, but during the past few years these regulations have been relaxed, and nowadays a registration by the target with a designated bank at its place of incorporation is sufficient. Upon completion of this registration, the seller may proceed to open the special account with the bank (which no longer needs to be at the location of seller's establishment).[187]

[245] In some locations, the local SAFE allows the opening of the special bank account to receive the purchase price only upon full completion of the transaction. In such case, payment can only be made after the necessary procedures to formalize the transaction have been completed. Since escrow arrangements are uncommon in China and often difficult to arrange, these restrictions do sometimes create a degree of risk to the seller.

[246] The purchase price is usually paid by the foreign buyer in foreign currency, which the local seller subsequently needs to convert into CNY. Previously, such conversion required SAFE approval (abolished in the course of 2012 and 2013) or

[185] Article 15 *2006 M&A Rules* requires the parties to disclose whether they are related, and if this is the case, the parties should provide evidence that the purchase price is at arm's length.

[186] Article 16 *2006 M&A Rules*.

[187] *2012 Forex FDI Circular; 2013 Forex FDI Provisions; 2015 Forex FDI Circular*.

SAFE registration (abolished in 2015). Nowadays, it is sufficient if the target completes the abovementioned registration with its bank.[188] Although less common, the purchaser may also elect to pay the purchase price by lawfully obtained CNY.[189]

4.2.2 Acquiring Part of a PRC Domestic-Owned Company

[247] Besides acquiring an *entire* domestic-owned company as described above, a foreign investor may also acquire *part* of the equity in a domestic-owned company, which results in the establishment of a joint venture with the remaining Chinese shareholder(s). Generally speaking, joint ventures are more difficult to operate than WFOEs, for several reasons. First, the former owner of the business remains in the picture, which may hinder attempts to operate the business in a way consistent with the foreign investor's usual operations. In practice, it is often difficult to curb the influence of the Chinese joint-venture partner over employees and vendors that are accustomed to following its directions. Second, joint ventures often have only a limited life span. There is a good chance that at some point – and often sooner rather than later – the joint-venture partners will differ in their opinions on the direction of the business, in which case, an exit may have to be negotiated. It is, therefore, important to spend sufficient time selecting the right partner, negotiating a good agreement and maintaining relationships throughout the term of the cooperation.

[248] Upon a foreign investor acquiring part of a domestic-owned company, the target company will become subject to all restrictions that foreign investors face, which mainly includes compliance with the *Foreign Investment Negative List* and restrictions on capitalization and foreign debt.

[249] The key regulatory difference between acquiring an *entire* domestic-owned company and only a *part*, thereof, is that in case of the former, the target converts into a WFOE (*see* above), while in case of the latter, the target converts into an Equity Joint Venture (EJV), since the equity will be held by both the foreign investor and its Chinese joint-venture partner (*see also* section 3.3.2 'Equity Joint Venture (EJV)'). However, once the *Foreign Investment Law* becomes effective in January 2020, conversion into an EJV will no longer occur, and from then, there will no longer be much difference between acquiring an entire company and only part thereof.

[250] An EJV is subject to several restrictions with respect to corporate governance (e.g., the board being the highest authority, mandatory veto rights), profit sharing and equity transfers (*see* further 3.3.2 'Equity Joint Venture (EJV)'). Furthermore, a PRC individual is generally not allowed to hold equity in an EJV (*see* [154]), but when such individual already holds equity in the target prior to it being converted into an EJV, such person may, subject to approval, continue to hold his equity.[190] Once the specific rules for EJV's are cancelled when the *Foreign Investment Law*

[188] *2012 Forex FDI Circular; 2013 Forex FDI Provisions; 2015 Forex FDI Circular.*
[189] Article 17, *2006 M&A Rules.*
[190] Article 54, 2006 M&A Rules.

becomes effective, these restrictions on PRC individuals regarding joint ventures with foreign parties are likely to be removed as well.

[251] The *2006 M&A Rules* and most other regulations discussed in the context of an entire acquisition (*see* section 4.2.1 'Acquiring an Entire PRC Domestic-Owned Company') will equally apply to a partial acquisition. For example, the transaction will be subject to the same foreign investment approvals and restrictions regarding price, payment terms and foreign exchange controls, while the equity purchase agreement needs to be governed by PRC law. In addition, the joint-venture contract also needs to be governed by PRC law and filed with MOFCOM when applying for approval of the transaction.[191]

4.2.3 Transferring Equity in an Foreign-Invested Enterprise

[252] Before, we only discussed equity transfers in domestic-owned enterprises (i.e., companies that only have Chinese shareholders). In case the equity in an Foreign-Invested Enterprise has to transfer, the rules are quite different. The *2006 M&A Rules* do not apply to the transfer of equity in an FIE, even if the target is an EJV and the seller is the Chinese joint-venture partner.[192] Instead, the *1997 FIE Acquisition Rules* and the *2016 FIE Filing Measures* apply, which contain much fewer restrictions compared to those under the *2006 M&A Rules* discussed above (section 4.2.1 'Acquiring an Entire PRC Domestic-Owned Company').

[253] As a result, parties have much more flexibility to agree on tailor-made solutions when it comes to the acquisition of an FIE. For example, there is no requirement that the purchase price should be based on an independent asset appraisal (although local tax authorities may still require this to determine applicable capital gains taxes), and there are no restrictions on when the purchase price should be paid, which allows for earn-outs and escrow arrangements. Moreover, in case the buyer and seller are both foreign investors, payment of the purchase price can be arranged offshore, so PRC foreign exchange restrictions will not affect the transaction either. The rules set forth in [244]–[246] do apply in case a Chinese party wishes to sell its stake in an EJV and needs to receive the purchase price in China.

[254] Since October 2016, the change of ownership of an FIE only requires a record-filing with MOFCOM if the company operates in an industry not included in the *Foreign Investment Negative List* (previously government approval was required). If the FIE's activities are restricted by the *Foreign Investment Negative List*, the transaction must still be approved by the competent local authorities, who may set specific requirements with regard to the terms and conditions of the transaction and the documents that must be submitted for approval and registration.[193]

[255] Regardless of whether the transfer of the equity in an FIE is subject to approval or only a record-filing, the authorities will check whether the transaction complies with the *Foreign Investment Negative List* (*see* [69]–[70]). This means that a

[191] Article 22 *2006 M&A Rules*; Art. 12 *1983 EJV Implementing Rules*; Art. 126(2) *Contract Law*.

[192] *2008 Foreign Investment Handbook*.

[193] Articles 2, 6 *2016 FIE Filing Measures*; Art 3 *1997 FIE Acquisition Rules*.

record-filing will be rejected if approval is required, and if the catalogue sets restrictions for the relevant industry, such restrictions should have been complied with (e.g., limits on foreign shareholding). If the FIE operates in a regulated industry, approval by the industry regulator may also be required, and if certain qualification criteria apply with respect to the (foreign) shareholder (*see* [47]), the foreign investor shall need to establish that it meets those criteria.[194]

[256] One strict condition imposed by the *1997 FIE Acquisition Rules* is the agreement of all the target company's investors if one of them wishes to transfer its equity. If the target company is an EJV, then the selling party must obtain the consent of, and assistance from, the parties that remain in the joint venture (*see also* [159]).[195] The Supreme Court has decided that this veto right will not be enforced if a party withholds its consent for an equity transfer but does not at the same time purchase the transferred equity under its right of first refusal as provided by the *Company Law* (*see* [143]). Local authorities, however, usually still require the signature of all other partners with reference to the *1997 FIE Acquisition Rules* and the *EJV Law* before they are willing to register an equity transfer. In practice, the cooperation of the joint-venture partners is, therefore, usually indispensable for any transfer of equity in an EJV.

[257] Note that once the *Foreign Investment Law* becomes effective in January 2020, foreign investors will start establishing regular PRC limited liability companies and companies limited by shares (*see* [132]), and after that, it is just a matter of time before foreign investors wish to transfer equity in those type of companies. At the moment, there is not yet a particular legal framework for such transactions, but it is expected that the rules and procedures will be quite similar to what has been discussed above regarding the *1997 FIE Acquisition Rules*.

4.2.4 Investments in Domestic-Owned Companies by Foreign-Invested Enterprises

[258] Until now we have only discussed scenarios where a foreign investor directly acquires equity in a PRC company. Instead, a foreign investor could also elect to incorporate an FIE first, or use an existing FIE, to acquire equity in a PRC company. If the target's equity is only held by domestic investors, such indirect acquisition will be subject to the *2000 FIE Investment Provisions*,[196] and not the (burdensome) *2006 M&A Rules* discussed above. In case the target's equity is (partly) held by foreign investors (i.e., the target itself is an FIE that will be acquired by another FIE), such transaction will also be subject to the *1997 FIE Acquisition Rules* described above.[197]

---

194 Articles 3, 4 *1997 FIE Acquisition Rules*; Art. 11 *2016 FIE Filing Measures*.

195 Articles 2, 9 *1997 FIE Acquisition Rules*; Art. 4 *EJV Law*.

196 These provisions have been subsequently amended by Art. 7 *2006 FIE Approval Opinions*, Art. 5 *2006 FIE Approval Opinions Interpretations* and Art. 2 *2015 FIE Registered Capital Decision*.

197 Article 15 *2000 FIE Investment Provisions*.

[259] If an FIE acquires a PRC company from domestic shareholders, such PRC company itself shall *not* convert into an FIE. The company will continue to be considered a domestic-owned entity, but on its business licence the authorities will mark that its shareholder is an FIE. The *2000 FIE Investment Provisions* do, nevertheless, require compliance with the *Foreign Investment Negative List* (*see* section 2.1.1 'The Foreign Investment Negative List'). An FIE may, therefore, not acquire any equity in a domestic enterprise that operates in any *prohibited* industry, while in case of a *restricted* industry, the FIE needs to comply with the relevant restrictions (e.g., limits on foreign ownership).[198]

[260] If an FIE acquires a domestic target that is active in an industry not in the *Foreign Investment Negative List*, the FIE only needs to make a record-filing with the AMR, and no MOFCOM approval or record-filing is required for the transaction. When an FIE intends to acquire a domestic-owned company that operates in a *restricted* industry, MOFCOM approval is, however, still required.[199]

[261] Previously, FIEs faced several restrictions when acquiring domestic-owned companies, but many of those restrictions have been lifted in recent years. For example, FIEs were not permitted to use their own registered capital to acquire domestic-owned companies, FIEs could invest no more than 50% of their net asset value in such companies, and FIEs were only allowed to acquire a domestic target after their own registered capital had been fully paid-up and they had commenced to make profits – these restrictions have all been removed.[200]

4.2.5 Offshore Transactions

[262] The most important reason to structure a transaction offshore is to avoid scrutiny from Chinese government officials. Many foreign investors route their investments into China through special purpose vehicles, and the sale of such an offshore holding company to another non-Chinese company or individual is generally not subject to Chinese laws or procedures (except maybe for capital gains taxes, *see* [267] below).

[263] Another benefit of an offshore transaction is that where the FIE is a joint venture, the transaction will not result in any transfer of equity in such joint venture, hence no approval of the joint-venture partners is required (*see* [256]) (unless, of course, the offshore shareholders' agreement contains any change of control provisions) nor will the statutory pre-emptive rights of the Chinese entity's other shareholders be triggered (*see* [143]).

[264] Foreign investors that wish to purchase another foreign-invested enterprise in China can thus acquire the equity of its holding company, a transaction that in most jurisdictions is straightforward and can be easily implemented without having

[198] Articles 3, 4, 15 *2000 FIE Investment Provisions*.

[199] Article 15 *2000 FIE Investment Provisions*.

[200] Article 7 *2006 FIE Approval Opinions*, Art. 5 *2006 FIE Approval Opinions Interpretations*, Art. 2 *2015 FIE Registered Capital Decision* and Art. 4 *2015 Forex Reform Circular*.

to conquer major obstacles. For the above reasons, structuring an equity transaction offshore is almost always the preferred option – though it is not feasible, of course, where the target company is domestically owned or where the holding company has other businesses that are not for sale.

[265] The sale of a holding company has some minor consequences to the Chinese subsidiary. For one, the legal representative, directors and supervisor (*see* [138]–[141]), all appointees of the original investor(s), will likely have to be replaced by appointees of the new owner. Also, it is common for the new controller to change the subsidiary's name and perhaps its corporate governance. But these procedures present little difficulty to the new investor, as long as it can count on the cooperation of the subsidiary and its existing management.

[266] The situation becomes more complicated if the foreign acquisition or merger affects competition in China. For large transactions that threaten to influence competition in the Chinese market, approval may also have to be obtained from China's anti-monopoly authorities (*see* section 4.8.6 'Merger Control').

[267] Minimizing tax liabilities may be a final reason to structure the transaction offshore. Many offshore jurisdictions have very friendly tax policies for transactions in their territory. Since the transaction takes place offshore and does not directly involve Chinese entities, it will usually not trigger taxes in China. However, there is one exception: where the foreign entity that is being transferred is considered an abusive use of commercial structure and serves no reasonable commercial purpose (e.g., an special purpose vehicle created specifically to hold the Chinse investment to avoid taxes in China), then PRC (capital gains) taxes will still be due.[201]

4.3 Subscription for New Equity

[268] Instead of acquiring equity from an existing shareholder, a foreign investor can also choose to subscribe for new equity by contributing additional registered capital to the target. This allows the target company to receive funds, which can be applied to further expand the business. Meanwhile, the existing shareholders will remain in place without the need to contribute to the registered capital increase – they retain their holdings based on their original shareholding, only at a lower proportion of the company's total equity.

[269] If a foreign investor subscribes for equity in a domestic-owned company (i.e., no foreign shareholding), the *2006 M&A Rules* apply, and upon issuance of the equity, the target shall convert into an FIE (although such conversion will no longer occur once the *Foreign Investment Law* becomes effective). The rules and procedures for the *subscription* of equity in a domestic-owned company are quite similar to what we have described above (sections 4.2.1 'Acquiring an Entire PRC Domestic-Owned

201 *2015 SAT Public Notice No. 7.*

Company'–4.2.2'Acquiring Part of a PRC Domestic-Owned Company') for the *transfer* of such equity.

[270] One difference is that although the subscription price for the increased registered capital should still be determined on the basis of the appraised value of the target company's existing equity, there are no fixed standards for such appraisal, and companies are generally allowed to arrange their own appraisals to meet their commercial needs (some local authorities may, however, still insist on receiving a formal appraisal report). In some cases, the appraisal will simply be based on the existing registered capital, while in others reference can be made to the present value of the company's assets, or to turnover and profits.[202]

[271] Another difference relates to the restrictions on the payment of the transaction price. Subject to agreement between the parties, the additional registered capital can be contributed by a foreign investor in the same way as a domestic investor would pay for an increase in registered capital, except that at a minimum, the foreign investor must pay 20% of its contribution to the company's capital account after approval and before registration with the AMR.[203]

[272] If a foreign investor subscribes for equity in a PRC target that already has foreign shareholders (i.e., the target is an FIE), the (burdensome) *2006 M&A Rules* do not apply. Instead, the transaction will be governed by the *1997 FIE Acquisition Rules* and the *2016 FIE Filing Measures*. The rules and procedures for the *subscription* of equity in an FIE are nearly the same as what we have described above (section 4.2.3 'Transferring Equity in an Foreign-Invested Enterprise') for the *transfer* of such equity, which means much fewer restrictions compared to subscribing for equity in a domestic-owned company.

[273] In [206], we set out that FIEs need to open a special capital account with the bank in order to be able to receive the subscription price from their investors when they issue equity. Previously, FIEs were required to register with SAFE before they could open such capital account, but since June 2015, SAFE has delegated this process and the registration can be done directly with certain designated banks.[204]

[274] Even though no specific rules allow foreign investors to contribute their subscription price in kind, it is generally understood that this is permitted. The same rules apply as those for contributing non-monetary assets to a newly established FIE (*see* [208]), which includes the requirement of an independent appraisal of the value of the contributed assets.

4.4 Share Swaps

[275] One of the new elements introduced by the *2006 M&A Rules* is the possibility of a share swap. Foreign investors are expressly permitted to use shares to pay for

[202] Article 17 *2006 M&A Rules*.

[203] Article 16 *2006 M&A Rules*.

[204] *2015 Forex FDI Circular; 2015 Forex Reform Circular.*

the purchase or subscription of equity in a domestic-owned company. The shares offered may be existing or newly issued shares but must be listed publicly on a lawfully existing overseas securities exchange (excluding OTC markets). Other conditions apply as well, including that the price of the offered shares in the year prior to the transaction has remained stable.[205]

[276] Equity acquisitions by means of a share swap are subject to approval from MOFCOM for the inbound part of the transaction (the foreign company's purchase of domestic equity), and from MOFCOM and SAFE with respect to the outbound part (the domestic company's purchase of foreign shares, as this qualifies as overseas investment by a domestic company). Moreover, before final approval has been obtained and SAFE has amended the company's registration, the target company may not pay dividends to its shareholders, provide a guaranty to any related company, nor make any payments for items under the capital account, such as an equity transfer, capital decrease or liquidation.[206]

[277] The first transaction under the *2006 M&A Rules* involving a share swap was only approved by MOFCOM in 2008, when Hong Kong-listed Poly (Hong Kong), Investments Limited acquired the entire equity interest in Shenzhen Poly Investments Co., Limited, from China Poly Southern Group Limited. However, few companies have since followed this example due to the cumbersome approval requirements for these transactions.

4.5 Asset Acquisitions

[278] One drawback to an equity acquisition, whether direct or indirect, is that the target company is acquired as a whole. This means that the purchaser will not only acquire the assets but also the company's debts and liabilities. In China, in particular, this presents a challenge no matter how complete a due diligence has been conducted on the target company. An alternative to the purchase of equity is to structure the transaction as an asset transaction. Under this type of acquisition, the purchaser cherry-picks those assets of the target company it finds desirable, while leaving behind the target's unwanted assets and liabilities.

[279] The *2006 M&A Rules* apply when a foreign investor acquires assets from a domestic-owned company, in which case these rules provide for two options: the assets can be purchased directly by the foreign investor and then contributed to a newly established company as registered capital, which is called an asset acquisition *with* establishment; or the investor first establishes a company, which then purchases the assets in question, which is referred to as an asset acquisition *after* establishment.[207] In either case, the new company will end up owning and operating the assets for its own account, without direct legal involvement of its foreign investor.

[205] Articles 28, 29 *2006 M&A Rules*.
[206] Articles 32–37 *2006 M&A Rules*.
[207] Article 2 *2006 M&A Rules*.

4.5.1 Terms & Conditions

[280] An asset acquisition is subject to similar restrictions on price as where domestic-owned equity is purchased: the transaction price of the assets shall be determined on the basis of an appraisal by a qualified appraisal institution (*see* [242]).[208]

[281] In case of an asset acquisition *with* establishment, the payment restrictions are also similar to those of an equity transfer: payment of the purchase price should be made in full within three months after the business licence of the new company is issued, except that if government approval is obtained, 60% of the transaction value can be paid within six months after the business licence has been issued with the balance to be paid within one year. In the event the asset transaction requires a cross-border payment of the purchase price, the same foreign exchange rules apply as set out above ([244]–[246]) with respect to equity transactions.[209]

[282] If the asset acquisition *after* establishment model is used, the payment restrictions are slightly different: the foreign investor needs to pay the new company at least such part of its capital contribution as is equal to the purchase price for the assets. This needs to be completed no later than the purchase price for the assets is due, to ensure that the new company will have sufficient funds to pay the seller on time.[210] Otherwise, the regular rules and foreign exchange restrictions for contributing capital to a newly established company apply (*see* section 3.5.1 'Registered and Paid-up Capital').

[283] In general, while the new company will acquire the rights, obligations and encumbrances (such as mortgages and liens) on the acquired assets, any liabilities of the seller unrelated to the assets will remain with the seller. Nevertheless, the *2006 M&A Rules* permit a foreign investor, the target company, the target company's creditors and other involved parties to reach an agreement on the settlement of the target company's rights and obligations, which should be submitted to the approval authorities for examination. In addition, at least fifteen days prior to the day that the foreign investor submits the application for the acquisition to the competent approval authorities, the target company is required to notify its creditors of the asset transaction and to issue a public notice in a newspaper.[211]

[284] The asset purchase agreement between buyer and seller has to be governed by PRC law,[212] and this agreement should of course comply with the *2006 M&A Rules* and other relevant rules and regulations. The relevant approval authorities will scrutinize the asset purchase agreement, and they have the power to request changes to this document.

---

[208] Article 14 *2006 M&A Rules*.

[209] Article 16 *2006 M&A Rules*.

[210] Article 16 *2006 M&A Rules*.

[211] Article 13 *2006 M&A Rules*.

[212] Article 24 *2006 M&A Rules*.

4.5.2 Procedures for Acquisition after Establishment

[285] Theoretically, one could argue that any purchase of assets by an existing company would be subject to the *2006 M&A Rules*, since this qualifies as an asset acquisition *after* establishment of the company. In practice, the law is, however, not applied this strict. There is little doubt that if a foreign-owned PRC company acquires land, buildings and/or all the machinery from a domestic enterprise, this transaction is subject to the *2006 M&A Rules* and requires approval. If such company only purchases part of another company's assets, while the seller continues to operate (part of) its own business, the general view is that this does not trigger the need for approval under the *2006 M&A Rules*.

[286] PRC law does, however, not provide conclusive guidance on this issue, so foreign investors should at all times make enquiries with the relevant local authorities on their position on a case-by-case basis. Some district-level departments of MOFCOM in Shanghai, for example, hold the view that their approval is only required for asset acquisitions *with* establishment – that is, any purchase of assets using capital that has been contributed directly by the shareholders is free from their supervision. In such an event, a foreign company can easily avoid the approval procedures by establishing a PRC company first, upon which such company purchases the assets without the direct involvement of the foreign investors.

4.5.3 Benefits & Drawbacks

[287] Bypassing existing liabilities of the target company makes the assets transaction comparatively safe and predictable and allows the prospective investor to avoid the need for an extensive due diligence investigation. Chinese companies generally have a lot of hidden liabilities; an acquisition of only the most valuable assets allows an acquirer to avoid most of the resulting risks. While a legal review of the target assets is still necessary, a due diligence of the seller is no longer a priority. This is not only useful in direct acquisitions but also where a foreign investor wants to establish a joint venture but is concerned about the Chinese party's existing liabilities.

[288] An asset acquisition has several major drawbacks as well. First, it is expensive, especially compared to an equity transaction. For example, value-added tax (VAT) is due over the transfer of the assets immediately upon purchase (although this can be credited later on if certain conditions are met). In case any land is transferred, land appreciation tax may be due as well. Second, the timeframe for completing the transaction is comparatively long because the acquired assets cannot be utilized before the new company is established. Third, where approval under the *2006 M&A Rules* is required, the seller must inform its creditors prior to the completion of the transaction. Finally, by only acquiring certain assets, the foreign investor leaves other valuable rights. Existing licences, for example, cannot be transferred, while the buyer can only take over commercial relations with their consent and cooperation.

[289] Note that in China there is no automatic transfer of employees in case of an asset transaction. The seller shall, therefore, have to terminate all employment contracts of employees who will transfer, while the purchaser needs to enter into a new contract with those employees. Employees usually only agree to such transfer if they receive sufficient severance from the seller, or if the purchaser is willing to explicitly recognize their previous years of service with the seller.

4.6 Mergers

[290] A merger between two Chinese companies whose equity is solely held by domestic shareholders is governed by the *Company Law* (and once the *Foreign Investment Law* enters into effect in January 2020, it is expected that mergers between regular Chinese companies owned by foreign investors will also be governed by the *Company Law*). Mergers that involve at least one FIE are regulated by the *2001 FIE Merger Regulations* – this, therefore, includes either an FIE merging with another FIE or an FIE merging with a company that only has domestic shareholders. It is not allowed for companies incorporated in the PRC to participate in a merger with companies established outside Mainland China.

[291] A merger is an option for those foreign investors that already have one or more FIE subsidiaries in China and intend to expand that business by acquiring another Chinese company. Such a merger is in fact quite similar to an equity acquisition, the only difference being the use of the Chinese FIE subsidiary as an investment vehicle. Another common use of the merger structure is where a foreign investor wishes to combine the business of two or more of its Chinese subsidiaries into one as part of a restructuring of its investments.

[292] After the merger of two or more existing entities has been completed, operations of the pre-merged companies will continue either through one of the merged companies (referred to as a *merger by acquisition*) or through a company newly established for this purpose (referred to as a *merger by consolidation*). The surviving or newly established entity, whether an EJV, CJV, WFOE or even an FICLS, will acquire all assets of the merged companies and succeed to their combined rights and liabilities.[213]

[293] The registered capital of the surviving or newly established entity after completion of a merger is usually equal to the sum of the registered capital of all pre-existing entities involved in the merger. The parties to the merger may either determine their relative equity holdings in the surviving or newly established entity by themselves and specify these ratios in their merger agreement and articles of association or they may choose to rely on an appraisal institute to determine the value of each party's contribution.[214]

[213] Articles 3, 25 *2001 FIE Merger Regulations*.
[214] Articles 11, 12 *2001 FIE Merger Regulations*.

[294] There is one exception to the rule above: in case a *limited liability company* and a *company limited by shares* merge *and* the surviving or newly established entity is the company limited by shares, the registered capital of such surviving or new company limited by shares shall be equal to the sum of (i) its own share capital; and (ii) the share capital derived by converting the net asset value of the limited liability company into shares on the basis of the net asset value per share of the company limited by shares.[215]

[295] When a company with foreign shareholders merges, the surviving or newly established entity should comply with the *Foreign Investment Negative List* – i.e., it is not allowed to operate in *prohibited* industries, and in case the company is active in a *restricted* industry, it should comply with the relevant limitations. In case the business scope of the surviving or new entity changes, approval must be sought, or a record-filing made, in accordance with the regular proceedings regarding the change of a company's business scope. Until 2015, only entities that had commenced business operations and whose registered capital had been fully paid-up were allowed to merge, but these restrictions have been lifted.[216]

[296] All companies involved in the merger should notify their respective creditors and publish a notice in a newspaper, announcing the merger and providing a proposal on the succession of their liabilities. These creditors have the right to demand amendments to the proposal or debt repayment prior to the merger, or alternatively the merged entities should provide sufficient security to protect the legitimate rights and interests of their creditors.[217]

[297] Even though the *2001 FIE Merger Regulations* require approval for all mergers involving an FIE, on the basis of the *2016 FIE Filing Measures*, it seems that a merger between two FIEs that operate outside the *Foreign Investment Negative List* no longer requires MOFCOM approval but only a record-filing (*see also* [63]). If at least one of the merging companies carries out activities restricted by the *Foreign Investment Negative List*, approval is still required in accordance with the *2001 FIE Merger Regulations*. Based on the *2016 Filing Measures*, it is unclear whether approval is required if an FIE merges with a domestic-owned company and both companies operate outside the scope of the *Foreign Investment Negative List*. Until there is more clarity, we recommend confirming this on a case-by-case basis with the relevant local authorities.[218]

[298] If the merger involving an FIE is subject to approval, pre-approval needs to be sought from the competent authorities of all merging entities involved prior to notifying the creditors. After expiry of the notification period for creditors, final approval for the merger needs to be obtained from the authority governing the surviving or newly established entity.[219]

[215] Article 11 *2001 FIE Merger Regulations*.
[216] Article 5 *2001 FIE Merger Regulations*; Art. 3 *2015 FIE Registered Capital Decision*.
[217] Articles 27–30 *2001 FIE Merger Regulations*.
[218] Articles 7, 8 *2001 FIE Merger Regulations*; Arts 2, 6 *2016 FIE Filing Measures*.
[219] Articles 7, 8, 22 *2001 FIE Merger Regulations*.

[299] Upon approval or acceptance of the record-filing (as applicable), the merged company shall complete de-registration formalities with customs, tax and AMR, which is usually quite time-consuming. The relevant tax authorities will review the company's tax situation and any identified liabilities, including CIT liabilities, will have to be paid before consent is given to move forward. Customs duties, if any, will have to be paid off first as well. In addition, if any assets are under customs supervision, customs approval may be sought to transfer the assets under customs supervision, or alternatively the entity may apply for the release of such assets from customs supervision against payment of supplemental duties.

[300] Upon de-registration of the merged companies, the surviving company can proceed to the competent AMR to amend its registration, or if a new company has been established, the new entity can apply for its initial business licence. Upon completion thereof, the surviving or new company shall notify all creditors and debtors of the dissolved companies of the merger and issue a public notice in a newspaper regarding the merger and the succession of liabilities and rights.[220]

[301] Besides resolving any outstanding tax issues of the companies involved in a merger, corporate income taxes may also be levied as a result of a merger. Unless the merger qualifies for any special tax treatment, this tax liability is usually calculated in accordance with the following principles. The surviving or newly established company shall determine the tax base of all assets and liabilities of any disappearing company on the basis of their fair value. A disappearing company and its shareholders shall subject themselves to corporate income tax as if the company was in liquidation. For example, if the book value of a disappearing company is CNY50m and the appraised value is CNY60m, then after the merger, the surviving or newly established company should book the assets as being worth CNY60m, while the difference (CNY10m) will be regarded as liquidation income of the disappearing company, which after the deduction of other losses shall be subject to corporate income tax. Any losses suffered by a disappearing company may, however, not be carried forward to the surviving or newly established company.

[302] Compared to an equity acquisition or asset acquisition, mergers are generally more complicated and burdensome from a regulatory perspective. However, the biggest, practical challenge to mergers is the need to deal with the multi-step approval or record-filing process that involves supervising authorities from both the merged and surviving or newly established entities. In China, the involvement of assorted government departments in different locations is a guarantee for complicated procedures, as these departments rarely work well together and are used to applying their own policies in handling applications. There is no legal reason why a merger involving an FIE cannot be completed, but considerable time must be spent on negotiating with officials and coordinating their decision-making. As a result, even in the face of necessary restructuring, many foreign investors will prefer to avoid a merger and instead prefer to arrange for a transfer of the business, followed by the liquidation of those structures that no longer serve any economic purpose.

[220] Articles 31–33, 36. 5 *2001 FIE Merger Regulations*.

4.7 Acquisition of State-Owned Assets

4.7.1 Introduction

[303] The acquisition of domestic-owned equity or assets is even more complicated if these are state-owned. Over the past two decades, the importance of State-Owned Enterprises (SOEs) in China's economy has gradually diminished with the private sector accounting for an ever-growing proportion of China's GDP. At the same time, whole sectors remain dominated by companies with a direct or indirect affiliation to governments at various levels. While China encourages foreign investors to participate in the restructuring of SOEs, at the same time, a special legal framework has been established to monitor M&A transactions involving state-owned assets to prevent the drain of these assets.

[304] In order to prevent state-owned equity or assets from being sold below their true value, PRC government has put several safeguards in place. The key pieces of legislation in this respect are the *State-Owned Assets Law* and the *2016 SOE Trading Measures*, while several other regulations provide more detailed guidance on a variety of topics.[221] The main regulator is State-owned Assets Supervision and Administration Commission (SASAC), which oversees and undertakes the shareholder's duties and rights of the more than one hundred centrally managed SOEs, while SASAC's various local branches are in charge of all other SOEs.[222]

[305] The above regulations do not make a distinction between foreign and domestic investors, so the relevant rules and regulations apply, in principle, equally to both of them, except that the *State-Owned Assets Law* states that any transfer of state-owned equity to an overseas investor should not compromise national security and public interest. The acquisition of equity or assets from an SOE by a foreign investor is of course still subject to the restrictions on foreign investment as set forth in the *Foreign Investment Negative List*. This means that foreign investors are not permitted to acquire the equity of an SOE operating in an industrial sector where foreign investment is *prohibited*, while certain conditions must be met if the sector is in the *restricted* category.[223]

[306] The *2016 SOE Trading Measures* regulate the following transactions: (i) a transfer of an SOE's equity, (ii) a capital increase of an SOE (unless only the PRC government subscribes for such increase), and (iii) a transfer of an SOE's major assets. For these purposes an SOE is defined as any company: (a) that is wholly owned by the State, (b) in which the State holds a (direct or indirect) majority stake, or (c) in which the State is the largest shareholder and over which the State is able to exercise control (e.g., on the basis of a shareholders' agreement).[224] Besides the

[221] *2005 SOE Valuation Measures*. The *2011 Central SOE Overseas Assets Measures* deal with overseas assets of the centrally managed SOEs, and in addition there are also several provincial and municipal regulations governing local SOEs.

[222] Articles 11–12 *State-owned Assets Law*; Art. 66 *Company Law*.

[223] Article 26 *2016 SOE Trading Measures*; Art. 57 *State-owned Assets Law*.

[224] Article 3–4 *2016 SOE Trading Measures*.

transactions above, the *State-Owned Assets Law* also governs mergers, spin-offs, the reduction of registered capital, the issuance of bonds, dissolutions and certain restructurings that involve SOEs.[225]

[307] Before completing any of the abovementioned transactions, several formalities must be *fulfilled*. The most important and common formalities are: (i) obtaining approval, (ii) an independent asset appraisal, and (iii) a public tender at a property exchange. We will discuss each of them in more detail below.

[308] Note that the transfer of financial institutions owned by the State are governed by different regulations, in which event the Ministry of Finance will be the main regulator instead of SASAC.[226] When it comes to listed SOEs, different rules apply as well; in which case, China Securities Regulatory Commission ('CSRC') will also play a role as regulator.

4.7.2 Obtaining Approval for the Transaction

[309] Since SASAC exercises the shareholder's duties and rights in SOEs on behalf of the State, any transfer of equity held by the State, therefore, by definition, requires SASAC's approval. In case of a wholly state-owned company, the *Company Law* provides that the SOE does not have a shareholders' meeting, and SASAC directly exercises all shareholders' rights, while each of the following transactions will require SASAC's approval: mergers, spin-offs, increases or decreases of registered capital, issuances of bonds and dissolutions.[227]

[310] In case the State has a controlling stake or is otherwise able to exercise control over an SOE, many of the transactions mentioned above will also require SASAC's approval, since these are decided by the shareholders or the board (over which SASAC will most likely have control).[228] Even in case of a minority stake, SASAC may still be able to block the transaction on the basis of statutory or contractual veto rights.[229]

[311] In the event that a transaction causes the State to lose control over an SOE, SASAC needs to submit such transaction to the government (at the same level as the competent SASAC authority) for approval. In the event of a merger, spin-off, dissolution or restructuring of a *significant* SOE over which the State has control, such government approval is also required.[230]

[312] An SOE itself is, in principle, free to decide on the transfer of its own major assets (e.g., land-use rights, real estate and production equipment), provided that it files its internal decision-making procedures and authorization limits with

[225] Chapter V *State-owned Assets Law*.

[226] *2009 SOE Financial Institutions Measures*.

[227] Article 66 Company Law; Art. 31 State-owned Assets Law

[228] Articles 32–33 State-owned Assets Law.

[229] *See* Arts. 43, 103, 121 *Company Law* for decisions that require a two-third majority (*see* further [142] above), and Arts. 32–33 *1983 EJV Implementing Rules* for mandatory veto rights in case of an EJV (*see* further [156] above).

[230] Articles 34, 40, 53 *State-owned Assets Law*; Arts 7, 34 *2016 SOE Trading Measures*.

SASAC.[231] An SOE is also authorized to exercise the shareholders' rights in its subsidiaries, and in that capacity an SOE may decide on equity transfers and capital increases of its subsidiaries. When it, however, comes to a subsidiary that operates in an important industry or key sector in relation to the national security or economy and such subsidiary is primarily responsible for important projects, SOEs still require SASAC's approval for any equity transfer or capital increase.[232]

[313] In case of a major transaction (e.g., equity transfer, merger, spin-off, restructuring, dissolution), an SOE needs to discuss this with, and solicit the views of, the relevant labour unions and the assembly of employee representatives.[233] In case an equity transfer or restructuring affects the interests of employees, the SOE needs to prepare a staffing plan, which should be discussed, adopted and approved by the assembly of employee representatives.[234]

4.7.3 Independent Asset Appraisal

[314] The following transactions involving state-owned assets or equity generally require an independent appraisal of the relevant equity or assets involved: equity transfers, mergers, spin-offs, certain restructurings, transfers of major assets, non-monetary capital contributions and dissolutions.[235]

[315] The appraisal needs to be carried out by a qualified institute, and the appraisal report, which is valid for one year, needs to be filed with the relevant authorities in order to be able to register completion of the transaction. In case the appraisal relates to any activities that require approval by the PRC government, the appraisal report itself also needs to be approved by SASAC (in addition to the SASAC approvals described above).[236]

[316] The appraised value of the equity or assets involved should form the basis for the final transaction price, and for equity transfers, this price shall, in principle, not be lower than 90% of the appraised value (also not in case of an auction, *see* further below), unless special approval has been obtained.[237]

[317] The requirement for an independent asset appraisal, however, generally does not apply when it comes to transferring listed equity, since prices will be based on the actual trading price of the relevant shares (but the approval procedures set out above still apply to such transfers).

[231] Articles 48–49 *2016 SOE Trading Measures*.

[232] Articles 8, 35 *2016 SOE Trading Measures*.

[233] Article 37 State-owned Assets Law.

[234] Article 41 State-owned Assets Law; Art. 10 *2016 SOE Trading Measures*.

[235] Articles 42, 47, 55 *State-owned Assets Law*; Arts 12, 38, 43 *2016 SOE Trading Measures*. *See also* Arts 6–7 *2005 SOE Valuation Measures* for certain other transactions requiring an asset appraisal, and for a few exceptions under which no appraisal is required.

[236] Articles 4, 9, 14, 17, 20, 21 *2005 SOE Valuation Measures*.

[237] Article 22 *2005 SOE Valuation Measures*.

4.7.4 Public Tender

[318] Transfers of state-owned equity, capital increases by SOEs, and the transfer of major assets by SOEs, in principle, all require that the equity or assets are publicly tendered through a duly established property rights exchange (there are numerous of these exchanges throughout China). Only upon completion of the tender procedure will the exchange issue a property right transaction certificate, which is the necessary document for the subsequent approval and completion of the transaction.[238]

[319] Detailed information on the proposed state-owned equity or assets has to be published in qualified newspapers and on the exchange's website for 10 to 40 working days (depending on the type of transaction), with the aim to solicit potential investors.[239] The seller of state-owned equity or assets may, in principle, not set any conditions with respect to the buyer. Exceptions to this rule are: (a) equity transfers in the event buyer qualifications are absolutely necessary, provided these conditions may not be targeted to a particular buyer nor create any hurdles for fair competition, and (b) capital increases by SOEs (i.e., the State remains a shareholder), in which case, the relevant SOE is permitted to set qualification criteria for potential investors.[240]

[320] In practice, it is common that before triggering the formalities of a transfer of state-owned equity or assets, the seller will have already reached an agreement with a prospective (foreign) investor, and the seller will, therefore, try to tailor the requirements to the prospective buyer. This is often condoned as long as the requirements comply with the above, are not ambiguous and do not contain unfair provisions that discriminate against other potential buyers.

[321] Upon expiry of the public solicitation period, if two or more prospective buyers are interested in the state-owned equity or assets, the seller should arrange an auction or bid process to determine with whom the transfer agreement will be signed. In case of a capital increase, more sophisticated methods like competitive negotiations or comprehensive evaluation are also permitted.[241] If there is only one offer, the parties involved may directly execute a binding transfer agreement.

[322] In case of an equity transfer, the base price during the public tender shall be at least equal to the appraised value of the equity, and this price may only be lowered when the offering does not result in any bids (by qualified bidders). The base price shall, however, at all times be at least 90% of the appraised value, unless special approval has been obtained.[242]

[323] The purchase price for any state-owned equity transfer should be paid in lump sum no later than five working days after completion of the transfer, except

[238] Articles 13, 39, 49, *2016 SOE Trading Measures*; *see* Arts. 31, 46 *2016 SEO Trading Measures* for circumstances where a non-public transfer is permitted.

[239] Articles 15, 39, 50 *2016 SOE Trading Measures*.

[240] Articles 14, 36, 39(7), 51 *2016 SOE Trading Measures*.

[241] Articles 22, 42 *2016 SOE Trading Measures*.

[242] Articles 17, 18 *2016 SOE Trading Measures*.

that in case of large amounts, the purchase price may be paid in instalments. In such case, the buyer needs to provide security and pay 30% of the total purchase price within five working days after completion, while the remainder, together with interest, should be paid within one year after completion. Any transfer by an SOE of its major assets should be paid in one lump sum.[243]

4.8 Government Approval for M&A Transactions

4.8.1 NDRC Approval or Record-Filing

[324] Submitting a project application report (in case approval is needed) or a record-filing to National Development and Reform Commission (NDRC) will be the first step in the regulatory approval process for an M&A transaction carried out by a foreign investor. This NDRC process has already been discussed in detail in section 2.4.1 'NDRC Approval or Record-Filing' above, so in this section, we limit ourselves to highlighting a few items relevant for M&A transactions.

[325] The following M&A transactions require either NDRC approval or a record-filing with NDRC: the merger or acquisition by a foreign investor of a domestic enterprise, subscriptions for new equity in a domestic enterprise by a foreign investor, capital increases by FIEs and FIEs investing in domestic-owned companies.[244]

[326] In section 2.4.1 'NDRC Approval or Record-Filing', we set out that NDRC approval is required if the relevant industry is listed in: (a) the *restricted* category of the *Foreign Investment Negative List,* or (b) sections 1–10 of the *Domestic Catalogue*. During its approval process, NDRC will carry out a substantive review of the project and the impact on resources, environment, economy and society (*see* further [58]). If no NDRC approval is required, the foreign investor needs to submit a simple record-filing with NDRC, that should also be accepted by NDRC, prior to carrying out the transaction ([61]).

4.8.2 MOFCOM Approval or Record-Filing

[327] If required, the most important step in almost all M&A transactions involving a foreign investor or an FIE is obtaining an approval certificate from Ministry of Commerce (MOFCOM) or its local commission of commerce at provincial, municipal or district level.[245] Without such approval certificate, it is often impossible to complete the transaction and make the required registrations with the relevant authorities.

[243] Articles 28, 52 *2016 SOE Trading Measures*.

[244] Article 2 *2014 NDRC Approval Rules* (the subscription for new equity by a foreign investor is not explicitly mentioned, but this will result in the formation of an EJV (*see* [248-250]), which is governed by these rules).

[245] Article 6 *2006 M&A Rules*; Art. 3 *1997 FIE Acquisition Rules*; Art. 9 *2000 FIE Investment Provisions*; Art. 7 *2001 FIE Merger Regulations*.

[328] MOFCOM approval is generally required, except for the following transactions:

(a) the transaction only involves FIEs active in industries outside the scope of the *Foreign Investment Negative List* – this only requires a record-filing with MOFCOM (for equity transfers *see* section 4.2.3 'Transferring Equity in an Foreign-Invested Enterprise' above, for equity subscriptions *see* [272] and for mergers *see* [297]);
(b) an offshore transaction that does not involve the transfer of any equity within the PRC – generally no PRC approval or filings required (*see* section 4.2.5 'Offshore Transactions' above); and
(c) an industry regulator has to approve the transaction instead of MOFCOM (*see* [339] below).

[329] It is not yet clear whether anything will change when the *Foreign Investment Law* becomes effective in January 2020. One could argue that since the law promises national treatment for industries outside the *Foreign Investment Negative List* (*see* [117]), no special record-filing should be required for those industries, but it remains to be seen whether this will indeed be implemented.

[330] Whether the application for approval needs to be submitted to central MOFCOM, or one of its provincial, municipal or district level departments, depends on the location, industry and amount of investment. The higher the level of the authority whose approval is required, the more complicated and time-consuming the process usually will be. Generally speaking, investments in industries not included in the *Foreign Investment Negative List* that have a transaction value of less than USD300m, and those projects in *restricted* sectors with a transaction value of less than USD50m, can be submitted to a local bureau of MOFCOM, while larger transactions should be approved by central MOFCOM.[246]

[331] Different rules apply to the different types of M&A transactions described in this chapter. Each of these rules defines the basic approval or record-filing process in a somewhat different way, but the procedures and application documents are nevertheless quite similar for each type of transaction. The main application documents for obtaining MOFCOM approval generally include:[247]

(a) an application form setting out the key details of the transaction;
(b) shareholder/board resolutions of the companies involved approving the transaction;
(c) notarized and legalized incorporation certificates of the foreign investors involved and passport copies of their authorized representatives;
(d) an evidence on the creditworthiness of the foreign investor(s);
(e) the audited accounts of the target company or companies involved;

[246] *2010 FIE Approval Delegation Circular*; *2009 Foreign Investment Approval Circular*, *2009 FIHC Approval Circular*, *2008 Foreign Investment Licensing Circular*, *2008 FIE Approval Delegating Circular*.

[247] For example, Arts 4, 21, 23, 26 *2006 M&A Rules*; Art. 9 *1997 FIE Acquisition Rules*; Arts 7, 9 *2000 FIE Investment Provisions*; Arts 5, 20 *2001 FIE Merger Regulations*.

(f) a valuation report of the target equity or assets by an independent asset appraisal institute;
(g) the main transaction document (e.g., equity purchase agreement, asset purchase agreement, equity subscription agreement, merger agreement);
(h) the proposed joint-venture contract in case of multiple investors (WFOE, EJV, CJV) or the promotor agreement (FICLS);
(i) the proposed articles of association and the business licence of each of the Chinese companies involved;
(j) a list of board members, supervisors, the legal representative and the general manager after completion of the transaction; and
(k) pre-approval from the industry regulator (if required) or documents showing compliance with relevant industry regulations (if MOFCOM need to consult with the industry regulator).

[332] Note that the above is only a general overview, and the specific requirements differ depending on the type of M&A transaction and the nature and value of the investment. An applicant should also at all times consult with the relevant department of MOFCOM prior to filing, since each local MOFCOM department has wide discretion (which is regularly exercised) to demand additional documents or require that documents are in a certain form. MOFCOM regularly rejects applications if it deems these are incomplete or not in the required form, but it is usually acceptable to cure such defects and resubmit an application later.

[333] MOFCOM scrutinizes the application documents and, depending on the type of transaction, may decide to reject an application if the transaction:[248]

(a) violates the principles of fairness, reasonableness, compensation of equal value and good faith (e.g., the authorities deem that the agreed terms are unfair towards the Chinese counterparty);
(b) may damage China's public interest;
(c) may harm the interest of creditors;
(d) has a major impact on China's economic security in case a foreign investor acquires control over a target: (i) in a key industry, (ii) that has influence on the state security, or (iii) that owns a well-known Chinese trademark or Chinese trade name;
(e) does not comply with the *Foreign Investment Negative List* (i.e., the relevant industry is *prohibited* for foreign investment, or if the industry is *restricted*, the relevant limitations have not been complied with); or
(f) violates any PRC laws or regulations (mainly in case the transaction involves state-owned assets or concerns a regulated industry).

[334] In practice, the key evaluation criteria is whether the application and transaction comply with all relevant PRC laws and regulations and MOFCOM's internal

[248] Articles 3, 4, 5, 12 *2006 M&A Rules* (does not mention condition c); Arts 3, 4 *1997 FIE Acquisition Rules* (does not mention conditions a and d); Arts 5, 6 *2001 FIE Merger Regulations* (does not mention conditions b, c and d); Art. 3 *2000 FIE Investment Provisions* (only mentions conditions e and f).

policies. Rejections on the basis of any of the other criteria are quite uncommon, although there are examples of cases where MOFCOM deemed the transaction terms unfair to the Chinese investor and demanded changes to address this.

[335] MOFCOM will scrutinize the transaction agreement, articles of association and the joint-venture contract (if any), and it is quite common for MOFCOM to require investors to make certain changes to these documents. The internal policies and requirements vary from location to location, and especially in more remote areas, officials are known to reject complex provisions in contracts due to their lack of experience therewith.

[336] In case only a *record-filing* with MOFCOM is required (i.e., the transaction only involves FIEs with business activities outside the *Foreign Investment Negative List*), the filing can be submitted online with the competent MOFCOM bureau. MOFCOM will check if the filing is complete and accurate, and whether the relevant transaction indeed only requires a record-filing. If there are no issues, MOFCOM will accept the record-filing online within three business days, and the applicant may collect a record-filing receipt. If the transaction falls outside the scope of the record-filing framework (e.g., the relevant industry is on the *Foreign Investment Negative List*), the filing will be rejected, while if the filing is deemed incomplete or inaccurate, the applicant will be granted a one-time fifteen business-day period to supplement the application.[249]

[337] The record-filing needs to be made within thirty days after the relevant shareholders or board have adopted a resolution approving the transaction.[250] In practice, however, local AMRs may require the record-filing receipt before they are willing to issue the new business licence or otherwise register the transaction (*see* section 4.8.7 'Post-approval Registrations' below), which means the record-filing may need to be done earlier than this thirty-day deadline.

4.8.3 Industry Regulator Approval

[338] In section 2.3 'Industry-Specific Restrictions', we discussed that more than a hundred business activities require additional industry-specific licensing, which may come with additional qualification criteria (e.g., minimum amount of assets owned by the foreign investor, minimum amount of registered capital of the FIE or a track record in the relevant industry). When an M&A transaction involves an entity that has a business scope that includes any of these regulated activities, approval from the relevant industry regulator is usually required (section 2.4.4 'Industry Regulator Approvals'). This approval process mainly involves a check whether all the qualification criteria for the licensed business scope have been met.

[339] As discussed above ([76]), industry regulator approval is usually connected to the general MOFCOM investment approval or record-filing in one of the following ways:

[249] Articles 7, 11, 12 *2016 FIE Filing Measures*.

[250] Article 6 *2016 FIE Filing Measures*.

(a) pre-approval from the industry regulator is required before submitting the transaction to MOFCOM for approval;
(b) MOFCOM seeks the opinion of the industry regulator (which can also be other departments of MOFCOM) during its own approval process;
(c) the industry regulator directly approves the foreign investment and no general approval by MOFCOM is required; or
(d) post-approval from the industry regulator is required after the MOFCOM approval or record-filing (and usually also after obtaining the business licence).

4.8.4 Approval for the Transfer of State-Owned Assets

[340] In case the transaction involves state-owned assets, the approval of State-owned Assets Supervision and Administration Commission (SASAC) is usually required, while other authorities may need to approve the transaction as well. We have described this process and the relevant criteria in detail in section 4.7.2 'Obtaining Approval for the Transaction' above.

4.8.5 National Security Review

[341] In section 2.4.5 'National Security Review', we have already described the *National Security Review* system in detail. In this section, we will only highlight a few key points. If the security review is required (not often the case), it will be conducted prior to the other approval procedures described above. Upon completion of the review, Chinese authorities may block a transaction, or require its terms to be amended if such transaction has impact on China's national security, economic stability or social order.

[342] Two types of M&A transactions by foreign investors are currently subject to review: (i) transactions in the military sector or targets related to China's national defence, and (ii) transactions resulting in a foreign investor *acquiring actual control* over a domestic target which has *bearing on national security* and is active in the area of *important* agricultural products, energy and resources, infrastructure, transport services, technology or equipment manufacturing (*see* [82] above for the definition of acquiring actual control).[251]

[343] There are three ways to initiate a national security review: (1) a voluntary filing by the foreign investor, (2) a local department of NDRC or MOFCOM reporting the transaction to central NDRC or MOFCOM (local MOFCOM usually becomes aware of a transaction when it is submitted to it for general investment approval), or (3) upon request by a third party (e.g., concerned government authorities, industrial associations, competitors, upstream/downstream businesses).[252]

[251] Article 1(1) *2011 Security Review Notice*.
[252] Article 1–3 *2011 Security Review Provisions*.

4.8.6 Merger Control

[344] Like other jurisdictions, China has, through the Anti-Monopoly Law and various supporting regulations and guidelines, implemented a merger control system. The system regulates the merger of undertakings; the acquisition of control over other undertakings through a share or asset transfer; and the acquisition of control over other undertakings, or the ability to exert a decisive influence on other undertakings, through contracts or otherwise.

[345] Under China's merger control system, transactions above certain notification thresholds must be submitted to the *Anti-monopoly Bureau of State* Administration for Market Regulation (SAMR) for anti-trust clearance. The relevant thresholds that trigger a merger clearance process are as follows:[253]

(1) the total worldwide turnover of all the business operators involved in the concentration exceeded CNY10bn in the previous financial year, and at least two of these operators each had a turnover in China that exceeded CNY400m in the previous financial year; or
(2) the total turnover in China of all business operators involved in the concentration exceeded CNY2bn in the previous financial year, and at least two of these operators each had a turnover in China that exceeded CNY400m in the previous financial year.

[346] When calculating the turnover to determine whether these thresholds are met, the entire group turnover is counted, including

- the relevant party itself;
- undertakings that are controlled (directly or indirectly) by the relevant party;
- undertakings that control (directly or indirectly) the relevant party;
- undertakings that are controlled (directly or indirectly) by undertakings that control the relevant party; and
- undertakings that are jointly controlled by two or more parties as specified above.

[347] Control should be determined based on not only legal elements such as the agreement of concentration and bylaws but also factual elements. The 2018 Guiding Opinions on Concentration Notification specifically mention that at least the below elements should be considered.[254] As some of these elements are quite vague, this gives SAMR a lot of discretion in determining control on a case-by-case basis:

- the purpose of the transactions and future plans;
- the equity structures and post-transaction equity changes;
- the items to vote and the voting mechanism of shareholders' meetings, the business operators' attendance rate and resolutions in the past;

[253] *2008 Merger Control Thresholds.*

[254] Article 3, *2018 Guiding Opinions on Concentration.*

- the structure and the voting mechanism of the board of directors and the board of supervisors;
- the appointment and dismissal of senior executives;
- the relationship between shareholders and directors of the acquired business operator, and whether there are votes by proxy or persons acting in concert; and
- whether there is a significant commercial relationship or a cooperation agreement among the controlling business operators and other business operators.

[348] The merger control system covers not only mergers and acquisitions, but also the establishment of joint ventures if the turnover of the parties involved reaches one of the above thresholds, and if at least two undertakings jointly *control* the joint venture. If a newly established joint venture is controlled by only one undertaking, then by definition a concentration of undertakings will not exist.[255]

[349] Before formal notification, parties to a transaction have the option of approaching SAMR for a pre-notification consultation. This consultation is particularly useful if the undertaking is believed not to meet the thresholds, but the involved parties want to be sure. In response, SAMR may provide guiding opinions on whether the proposed transaction must be notified; what documents and information are required as part of the notification; and specific legal and factual issues, such as definition of the relevant market.

[350] There are two kinds of formal notifications – a full notification and a simplified one. The simplified notification is much quicker and is meant for transactions that are unlikely to restrict competition but meet the relevant thresholds for a filing. Specifically, only one of the following criteria must be met to qualify for a simplified notification:

(a) The combined market shares of all undertakings involved in the concentration in the same relevant market are less than 15% in total.
(b) The market shares of the undertakings involved in the concentration, which have a vertical relationship, are less than 25% in the upstream and downstream markets.
(c) The market shares of the undertakings involved in the concentration, which neither operate in the same relevant market nor have a vertical relationship, are less than 25% in each market related to the transaction.
(d) The undertakings involved in the concentration establish a joint venture outside China which does not engage in business activities in China.
(e) The undertakings involved in the concentration acquire shares or assets of overseas companies, which do not engage in business activities in China.
(f) A joint venture jointly controlled by two or more undertakings will be controlled by one or more undertakings through the concentration.

[255] Article 4, *2018 Guiding Opinions on Concentration.*

[351] If none of the above circumstances apply, then a full review is in order. From a procedural perspective, this includes a preliminary review which usually takes one to two months upon submission and then a substantive review. The simplified notification process stops upon completion of the preliminary review, presuming that SAMR approves the transaction. For the preliminary review process, SAMR only accepts *executed* transaction documents while implementation of the transaction is conditional upon approval, and so transaction documents will need to include clauses conditioning effectiveness upon completion of SAMR's review.

[352] Whether SAMR approves a transaction depends on whether it finds that the transaction will have negative competitive effects. Focus points are: the market shares of the parties or their power in the relevant market; the existing level of concentration in the relevant market; the implications that the transaction may have for new market entries or the development of technology; the impact of the transaction on consumers and other business operators; and the impact it may have on the national economy.

[353] Where SAMR finds that a transaction may restrict competition, the involved parties can take the initiative to negotiate changes to the transaction that can satisfy SAMR. If remedies are not introduced to SAMR's satisfaction, then it can order the parties to not implement the transaction; the disposal of certain shares or assets, of part of the business; and SAMR can issue a fine of CNY500 000. Meanwhile, if SAMR concludes that a transaction should have been notified as per current thresholds but the parties failed to submit a notification, then SAMR can also fine the parties for CNY500 000 and order the unwinding of the transaction. A notable trend in recent years is the increase of the number of investigations into transactions that have not been notified for merger review. That China is serious about combatting monopolies can also be seen from the very recent promulgation of three sets of regulations of SAMR on enforcing China's anti-trust laws.[256]

4.8.7 Post-approval Registrations

[354] After obtaining all relevant approvals, the next procedural step of a transaction is registration with SAMR or, more commonly, with a local AMR at provincial, municipal or district level. This involves not only the change of ownership but also other corporate changes, such as to the company name, the articles of association, or the board of directors. All of these details are registered with the competent AMR. Upon examination and registration, AMR will issue the company's amended business licence or a new business licence (in case of an asset transaction *with* establishment or a merger by *consolidation*), which marks the formal completion of the M&A transaction.

[355] We note that in case only a record-filing with MOFCOM is required, both the *2016 FIE Filing Measures* (issued by MOFCOM) and the *2016 FIE Filing Circular* (issued by SAMR) allow for the possibility to obtain a business licence with AMR

[256] *2019 Prohibiting Monopoly Agreements Provisions; 2019 Prohibitions on Abusing Market Dominance; 2019 Prohibitions on Abusing Administrative Power in Competition.*

first and complete the record-filing with MOFCOM within thirty days thereafter.[257] In practice, however, many local AMRs require the record-filing receipt issued by MOFCOM to be submitted to them before they are willing to issue the business licence.

[356] In addition to AMR registration, various post-formation registrations and bank information need to be updated accordingly and normally can be done within two to three weeks after the amended or new business licence is issued. In case of a cross-border payment of the purchase price, the target needs to register the transaction with a qualified bank, and the seller needs to open a special bank account to receive the purchase price (*see* [244]–[246] above).

[257] Article 11 *2016 FIE Filing Measures*; Art. 3 *2016 FIE Filing Circular*.

SHORT-FORM REFERENCES TO PRC LAWS & REGULATIONS

A. List of PRC Laws

Laws are referred to by using an unofficial short-form English name. The full name and other details of the relevant PRC laws can be found in the table below.

Short-Form English Name	*Full English Name*	*Full Chinese Name*	*Issued (d/m/y)*	*Effective (d/m/y)*	*Last Amended*	*Issued By*
Anti-Monopoly Law	Anti-Monopoly Law	中华人民共和国反垄断法	30/8/2007	01/08/2008		NPC Standing Committee (*2007/68*)
CIT Law	Corporate Income Tax Law	中华人民共和国企业所得税法	16/03/2007	01/01/2008	29/12/2018	NPC (*2018/23*)
CJV Law	Law on Chinese-Foreign Contractual Joint Ventures	中华人民共和国中外合作经营企业法	13/04/1988	13/04/1988	5/11/2017	NPC Standing Committee (*2017/81*)
Company Law	Company Law	中华人民共和国公司法	29/12/1993	01/07/1994	26/10/2018	NPC Standing Committee (*2018/15*)
Contract Law	Contract Law	中华人民共和国合同法	15/3/1999	01/10/1999		NPC (*1999/15*)
EJV Law	Law on Chinese-Foreign Equity Joint Ventures	中华人民共和国中外合资经营企业法	08/07/1979	08/07/1979	1/10/2016	NPC Standing Committee (*2016/51*)
Foreign Investment Law	Foreign Investment Law of the People's Republic of China	中华人民共和国外商投资法	15/03/2019	01/01/2020		NPC(2019/26)

Short-Form English Name	*Full English Name*	*Full Chinese Name*	*Issued (d/m/y)*	*Effective (d/m/y)*	*Last Amended*	*Issued By*
Individual Proprietorship Law	Law on Individual Proprietorship Enterprises	中华人民共和国个人独资企业法	30/08/1999	01/01/2000		NPC Standing Committee (*1999/20*)
National Security Law	National Security Law	中华人民共和国国家安全法	01/07/2015	01/07/2015		NPC Standing Committee (*2015/29*)
Partnership Law	Partnership Enterprise Law	中华人民共和国合伙企业法	23/02/1997	01/08/1997	27/08/2006	NPC Standing Committee (*2006/55*)
Securities Law	Securities Law	中华人民共和国证券法	29/12/1998	01/07/1999	31/08/2014	NPC Standing Committee (*2014/14*)
State-Owned Assets Law	Law on State-Owned Assets of Enterprises	中华人民共和国企业国有资产法	28/10/2008	01/05/2009		NPC Standing Committee (*2008/5*)
WFOE Law	Law of the People's Republic of China on Wholly Foreign-Owned Enterprises	中华人民共和国外资企业法	12/04/1986	12/04/1986	01/10/2016	NPC Standing Committee (*2016/51*)

B. List of PRC Rules & Regulations

PRC rules & regulations are referred to by using an unofficial short-form English name. The full name and other details of the relevant PRC rules & regulations can be found in the table below.

Short-Form English Name	*Full English Name*	*Full Chinese Name*	*Issued (d/m/y)*	*Effective (d/m/y)*	*Last Amended*	*Issued By*
1980 Rep Office Regulations	Interim Regulations Concerning the Control of Resident Offices of Foreign Enterprises	中华人民共和国国务院关于管理外国企业常驻代表机构的暂行规定	30/10/1980	30/10/1980		State Council (*GuoFa 1980/272*)
1983 EJV Implementing Rules	Rules for the Implementation of the Law on Chinese-Foreign Equity Joint Ventures	中华人民共和国中外合资经营企业法实施条例	20/09/1983	20/09/1983	02/03/2019	State Council (*2019/709*)
1987 FIE Registered Capital Regulations	Provisional Regulations for the Proportion of Registered Capital to Total Amount of Investment of Joint Ventures Using Chinese and Foreign Investment	国家工商行政管理局关于中外合资经营企业注册资本与投资总额比例的暂行规定	17/02/1987	17/02/1987		SAMR (*GongShangQiZi 1987/38*)
1990 EJV Contract Term Provisions	Interim Provisions Concerning Contract Period of Chinese-Foreign Equity Joint Ventures	中外合资经营企业合营期限暂行规定	22/10/1990	22/10/1990	08/01/2011	State Council (*2011/588*)
1990 WFOE Implementing Rules	Rules for the Implementation of the Law on Foreign-Funded Enterprises	中华人民共和国外资企业法实施细则	12/12/1990	12/12/1990	19/02/2014	State Council (*2014/648*)

Short-Form English Name	*Full English Name*	*Full Chinese Name*	*Issued (d/m/y)*	*Effective (d/m/y)*	*Last Amended*	*Issued By*
1991 WFOE Law Interpretation	The Interpretation of Several Provisions of Rules for the Implementation of the Law on Foreign-Funded Enterprises	对外经济贸易部关于发布《关于<中华人民共和国外资企业法实施细则>若干条款的解释》的通知	06/12/1991	06/12/1991		MOFTEC (*WaiJingMaoFa 1991/760*)
1995 CJV Implementing Rules	Rules for the Implementation of the Law on Chinese-Foreign Contractual Joint Ventures	中华人民共和国中外合作经营企业法实施细则	04/09/1995	04/09/1995	01/03/2017	State Council (*2017/676*)
1995 FICLS Rules	Provisional Regulations on the Establishment of Foreign-Funded Joint Stock Companies Limited	关于设立外商投资股份有限公司若干问题的暂行规定	10/01/1995	10/01/1995	28/10/2015	MOFCOM (*2015/2*)
1995 FIE Registered Capital Adjustment Circular	Circular on the Provision and Procedures Concerning Adjustment of the Proportion of an FIE's Registered Capital to Total Amount of Investment	对外贸易经济合作部、国家工商行政管理局关于外商投资企业调整投资总额和注册资本有关规定及程序的通知	25/05/1995	25/05/1995		MOFTEC and SAMR (*WaiJing-MaoFaFa 1995/366*)
1996 CJV Implementing Rules Interpretation	Circular on Implementing Certain Articles of the Rules for the Implementation of the Law on Chinese-Foreign Contractual Joint Ventures	对外贸易经济合作部关于发布《关于执行<中华人民共和国中外合作经营企业法实施细则>若干条款的说明》的通知	22/10/1996	22/10/1996		MOFTEC (*WaiJingMaoFa 1996/658*)
1996 Forex Settlement Regulation	Administrative Regulation regarding Foreign Exchange Settlement, Sales and Payment	结汇、售汇及付汇管理规定	20/06/1996	01/07/1996		PBOC (*YinFa 1996/210*)

Short-Form English Name	*Full English Name*	*Full Chinese Name*	*Issued (d/m/y)*	*Effective (d/m/y)*	*Last Amended*	*Issued By*
1997 FIE Acquisition Rules	Provisions for the Alteration of Investors' Equities in Foreign-Funded Enterprises	对外贸易经济合作部、国家工商行政管理局关于印发《外商投资企业投资者股权变更的若干规定》的通知	28/05/1997	28/05/1997		MOFTEC and SAMR (*WaiJing-MaoFaFa 1997/267*)
2000 FIE Investment Provisions	The Interim Provisions on the Domestic Investment of Foreign-Funded Enterprises in China	关于外商投资企业境内投资的暂行规定	25/07/2000	01/09/2000	28/10/2015	MOFCOM (*2015/2*)
2000 FIE Medical Institutions Interim Measures & Supplementary Provisions	Interim Measures for the Administration of Chinese-Foreign Equity Joint and Cooperative Joint Medical Institutions	中外合资、合作医疗机构管理暂行办法及其补充规定	15/05/2000	01/07/2000	01/01/2009	MOFTEC and MOH (*2000/11*)
2001 FICLS Circular	Circular on Relevant Issues of Joint Stock Companies with Foreign Investment	对外贸易经济合作部办公厅关于外商投资股份公司有关问题的通知	17/05/2001	17/05/2001		MOFTEC (*WaiJingMaoZiZi 2001/39*)
2001 FIE Merger Regulations	Regulations on the Merger and Division of Foreign-Invested Enterprises	关于外商投资企业合并与分立的规定	22/11/2001	22/11/2001	28/10/2015	MOFCOM (*2015/2*)
2001 Foreign Investment in Listed Companies Opinions	Opinions Relevant to Foreign Investment in Listed Companies	对外贸易经济合作部、中国证券监督管理委员会关于印发《关于上市公司涉及外商投资有关问题的若干意见》的通知	08/10/2001	08/10/2001		MOFTEC and CSRC (*WaiJing-MaoZiFa 2001/538*)
2001 Regulations on Foreign Law Firms	Administrative Regulations on the China-Based Representative Offices of Foreign Law Firms	外国律师事务所驻华代表机构管理条例	22/12/2001	01/01/2002		State Council (*2001/338*)

Short-Form English Name	*Full English Name*	*Full Chinese Name*	*Issued (d/m/y)*	*Effective (d/m/y)*	*Last Amended*	*Issued By*
2002 FIE Construction Measures	The Measures for the Administration of Foreign-Invested Construction Enterprises	外商投资建筑业企业管理规定	27/09/2002	01/12/2002		Ministry of Construction and MOFTEC (*2002/113*)
2002 Foreign Law Firms Implement Provisions	Provisions of the Ministry of Justice on the Implementation of the Administrative Regulations on the China-Based Representative Offices of Foreign Law Firms	司法部关于执行《外国律师事务所驻华代表机构管理条例》的规定	04/07/2002	01/09/2002	21/12/2018	Ministry of Justice (2018/10)
2002 Investment Catalogue Guidelines	Regulations on Guidelines of Foreign Investment Directions	指导外商投资方向规定	11/02/2002	01/04/2002		State Council (*2002/346*)
2002 Public Takeover Measures	The Administrative Measures for the Acquisition of Listed Companies	上市公司收购管理办法	28/9/2002	001/12/2002	23/11/2014	CSRC (*2014/108*)
2003 FIE Construction Implementing Rules	Implementing Rules for the Relevant Administration of Qualifications in the Administration of Foreign-Invested Construction Enterprises	建设部关于印发《建设部关于外商投资建筑业企业管理规定中有关资质管理的实施办法》的通知	08/04/2003	08/04/2003		Ministry of Construction (*JianShi 2003/73*)
2003 FIE Strengthening Circular	Circular Concerning the Relevant Issues on Strengthening the Approval, Registration, Foreign Exchange Control and Taxation Administration of Foreign-Funded Enterprises	对外贸易经济合作部、国家税务总局、国家工商行政管理总局、国家外汇管理局关于加强外商投资企业审批、登记、外汇及税收管理有关问题的通知	30/12/2002	01/01/2003		MOFTEC, SAT, SAMR, and SAFE (*WaiJingMaoFaFa 2002/575*)

Short-Form English Name	*Full English Name*	*Full Chinese Name*	*Issued (d/m/y)*	*Effective (d/m/y)*	*Last Amended*	*Issued By*
2003 Foreign Debt Management Measures	Interim Measures on the Management of Foreign Debts	外债管理暂行办法	08/01/2003	01/03/2003		NDRC, MOF, and SAFE (*2003/28*)
2003 Sino-Foreign Education Regulations	Regulations on Sino-foreign Cooperative Education	中外合作办学条例	01/03/2003	01/09/2003	02/03/2019	State Council (*2019/709*)
2004 Decisions of Amending FLF Regulations	Decisions of the Ministry of Justice on Amending the Administrative Regulations on the China-Based Representative Offices of Foreign Law Firms	司法部关于修改《司法部关于执行<外国律师事务所驻华代表机构管理条例>的规定》的决定	02/09/2004	02/09/2004		Ministry of Justice(2004/92)
2004 Enterprise Name Implementation Measures	Measures for the Implementation of the Administration of Enterprise Name Registration	企业名称登记管理实施办法（2004年修订）	14/06/2004	01/07/2004		AMR (*2004/10*)
2004 FIHC Provisions	Provisions on the Establishment of Investment Companies by Foreign Investors	商务部关于外商投资举办投资性公司的规定(2004二次修订)	17/11/2004	17/12/2004	28/10/2015	MOFCOM (*2015/2*)
2004 Hazardous Wastes Measures	The Measures for the Administration of Permit for Operation of Hazardous Wastes	危险废物经营许可证管理办法	30/05/2004	01/07/2004	06/02/2016	State Council (*2016/666*)
2004 SFER Implement Measures	Implementing Measures for the Regulations of the People's Republic of China on Sino-Foreign Cooperative Education	中华人民共和国中外合作办学条例实施办法	06/02/2004	01/07/2004		Ministry of Education (2004/20)

Short-Form English Name	*Full English Name*	*Full Chinese Name*	*Issued (d/m/y)*	*Effective (d/m/y)*	*Last Amended*	*Issued By*
2005 FIE Freight Transportation Measures	Administrative Measures for Foreign-Funded International Freight Transportation Agency Enterprises	外商投资国际货物运输代理企业管理办法	01/12/2005	11/12/2005	28/10/2015	MOFCOM (*2015/2*)
2005 Foreign Strategic Investment Measures	Administrative Measures for Strategic Investment in Listed Companies by Foreign Investors	外国投资者对上市公司战略投资管理办法	31/12/2005	30/1/2006	28/10/2015	MOFCOM (*2015/2*)
2005 SOE Valuation Measures	Interim Measures for the Administration of Assessment of State-Owned Assets of Enterprises	企业国有资产评估管理暂行办法	25/08/2005	25/08/2005		SASAC (*2005/12*)
2005 Split Share Structure Measures	Administrative Measures on the Split Share Structure Reform of Listed Companies	中国证券监督管理委员会关于发布《上市公司股权分置改革管理办法》的通知	04/09/2005	04/09/2005		CSRC (*ZhengJianFa 2005/86*)
2006 FIE Approval Opinions	Circular on Printing and Issuing Suggestions on Implementation of Several Issues Applicable for Application of the Law Governing the Approval and Registration of Foreign-Invested Companies	国家工商行政管理总局、商务部、海关总署、国家外汇管理局关于印发《关于外商投资的公司审批登记管理法律适用若干问题的执行意见》的通知	24/04/2006	24/04/2006		MOFCOM, SAMR, SAFE, GAC (*GongShangWai QiZi 2006/81*)

Short-Form English Name	*Full English Name*	*Full Chinese Name*	*Issued (d/m/y)*	*Effective (d/m/y)*	*Last Amended*	*Issued By*
2006 FIE Approval Opinions Interpretations	Interpretation of the Key Clauses in the 'Circular on Printing and Issuing Suggestions on Implementation of Several Issues Applicable for Application of the Law Governing the Approval and Registration of Foreign-Invested Companies'	国家工商总局外资局发布《关于外商投资的公司审批登记管理法律适用若干问题的执行意见》重点条款解读	22/09/2006	22/09/2006		SAMR
2006 Foreign-invested Banks Regulations	Administrative Regulations on Foreign-Invested Banks	中华人民共和国外资银行管理条例	11/11/2006	11/12/2006	27/11/2014	State Council (*2014/657*)
2006 M&A Rules	Provisions on M&A of a Domestic Enterprise by Foreign Investors	关于外国投资者并购境内企业的规定	08/08/2006	08/09/2006	22/06/2009	MOFCOM (*2009/6*)
2006 QFII Measures	Administrative Measures for Qualified Foreign Institutional Investors in Domestic Securities Investment	合格境外机构投资者境内证券投资管理办法	24/08/2006	01/09/2006		CSRC, PBOC, and SAFE (*2006/36*)
2006 RAFII Administrative Measures	Administrative Measures for the Representative Agencies of Foreign Insurance Institutions in China (2006)	外国保险机构驻华代表机构管理办法（2006年）	12/07/2006	01/08/2016	13/02/2018	China Insurance Regulatory Commission (2006/5)
2006 Supplementary FIHC Provisions	Supplementary Provisions on the Establishment of Investment Companies by Foreign Investors	关于外商投资举办投资性公司的补充规定	26/05/2006	01/07/2006	28/10/2015	MOFCOM (*2015/2*)

Short-Form English Name	*Full English Name*	*Full Chinese Name*	*Issued (d/m/y)*	*Effective (d/m/y)*	*Last Amended*	*Issued By*
2008 FIE Approval Delegating Circular	Circular on Delegating Matters Concerning the Changes to, and Examination and Approval of, Foreign-Invested Companies Limited by Shares and Enterprises	商务部关于下放外商投资股份公司、企业变更、审批事项的通知	5/08/2008	11/08/2008		MOFCOM (*ShangZiHan 2008/50*)
2008 FIE Telecom Enterprises Provisions	Provisions on the Administration of Foreign-Funded Telecommunications Enterprises	外商投资电信企业管理规定	10/09/2008	10/09/2008	06/02/2016	State Council (*2016/666*)
2008 Foreign Investment Handbook	Foreign Investment Market Entry Administrative Guidance Handbook	关于下发《外商投资准入管理指引手册》（2008年版）的通知	18/12/2008	18/12/2008		MOFCOM (*ShangZiFuZi 2008/530*)
2008 Foreign Investment Licensing Circular	Circular on Further Simplifying and Regulating Administrative Licensing of Foreign Investment	商务部关于进一步简化和规范外商投资行政许可的通知	26/08/2008	26/08/2008		MOFCOM (*ShangZiHan 2008/21*)
2008 Forex Control Regulations	Regulations of the PRC on Foreign Exchange Control	中华人民共和国外汇管理条例（2008年修订）	05/08/2008	05/08/2008		State Council (*2008/532*)
2008 Merger Control Thresholds	Provisions on the Standard for Declaration of Concentration of Business Operators	国务院关于经营者集中申报标准的规定	03/08/2008	03/08/2008	18/09/2018	State Council (*2018/703*)

Short-Form English Name	*Full English Name*	*Full Chinese Name*	*Issued (d/m/y)*	*Effective (d/m/y)*	*Last Amended*	*Issued By*
2009 FI Financial Information Services Administrative Provision	Administrative Provisions on Rendering of Financial Information Services by Foreign Institutions within the Territory of China	外国机构在中国境内提供金融信息服务管理规定	30/04/2009	01/06/2009		State Council, SAMR and Ministry of Commerce (2009/7)
2009 FIHC Approval Circular	Circular on Delegating the Authority to Approval the Establishment of Investment Companies by Foreign Investors	商务部关于下放外商投资举办投资性公司审批权限的通知	06/03/2009	06/03/2009		MOFCOM (*ShangZiHan 2009/8*)
2009 FIP Measures	Administrative Measures for the Establishment of Partnership Enterprises within China by Foreign Enterprises or Individuals	外国企业或者个人在中国境内设立合伙企业管理办法	25/11/2009	01/03/2010		State Council (*2009/567*)
2009 Food Safety Regulations	Implementing Regulations of the Food Safety Law	中华人民共和国食品安全法实施条例	20/07/2009	20/07/2009	06/02/2016	State Council (*2016/666*)
2009 Foreign Investment Approval Circular	Circular on Further Improving the Examination and Approval of Foreign Investment	商务部关于进一步改进外商投资审批工作的通知	05/03/2009	05/03/2009		MOFCOM (*ShangZiHan 2009/7*)
2009 Non-cash Contribution Notice	Notice on Several Issues Concerning Strengthening Management of Appraisal on Capital Contributions Made in Non-monetary Properties	财政部、工商总局关于加强以非货币财产出资的评估管理若干问题的通知	30/03/2009	30/03/2009		MOF and SAMR (*CaiQi 2009/46*)

Short-Form English Name	*Full English Name*	*Full Chinese Name*	*Issued (d/m/y)*	*Effective (d/m/y)*	*Last Amended*	*Issued By*
2009 SOE Financial Institutions Measures	Measures for the Administration of the Transfer of State-Owned Assets of Financial Enterprises	金融企业国有资产转让管理办法	17/03/2009	01/05/2009		Ministry of Finance (*2009/54*)
2010 FIE Approval Delegation Circular	Circular on Delegating Approval Authority over Foreign Investment to Local Counterparts	商务部关于下放外商投资审批权限有关问题的通知	10/06/2010	10/06/2010		MOFCOM (*ShangZiFa 2010/209*)
2010 FIE Disputes Provisions	Provisions on Several Issues Concerning the Hearing of Cases about Disputes Involving Foreign-Funded Enterprises (I)	最高人民法院关于审理外商投资企业纠纷案件若干问题的规定（一）	05/08/2010	16/08/2010		Supreme People's Court (*FaShi 2010/9*)
2010 FIIC Implement Rules	Implementing Rules for the Administrative Regulations of the People's Republic of China on Foreign-Invested Insurance Companies (Revised in 2010)	中华人民共和国外资保险公司管理条例实施细则（2010年修订）	03/12/2012	03/12/2012	13/02/2018	China Insurance Regulatory Commission (2010/10)
2010 FIP Registration Provisions	Provisions on the Administration of Registration of Foreign-Invested Partnership Enterprises	外商投资合伙企业登记管理规定	29/1/2010	01/03/2010	08/08/2019	SAMR (*2019/14*)
2010 Rep Office Tax Collection Interim Measures	Interim Measures for the Administration of Tax Collection against the Permanent Representative Offices of Foreign Enterprises	关于印发《外国企业常驻代表机构税收管理暂行办法》的通知	20/02/2010	01/01/2010	15/06/2018	State Administration of Taxation (*2018/31*)

Short-Form English Name	*Full English Name*	*Full Chinese Name*	*Issued (d/m/y)*	*Effective (d/m/y)*	*Last Amended*	*Issued By*
2011 Central SOE Overseas Assets Measures	Interim Measures for the Administration of the Overseas State-owned Property Rights of Central State-Owned Enterprises	中央企业境外国有产权管理暂行办法	14/06/2011	01/07/2011		SASAC (*2011/27*)
2011 RO Registration Regulations	Regulation on the Administration of Registration of Resident Representative Offices of Foreign Enterprises	外国企业常驻代表机构登记管理条例	19/11/2010	01/03/2011	18/09/2018	State Council (*2018/703*)
2011 Security Review Notice	Notice on the Establishment of the Security Review System for Mergers and Acquisitions of Domestic Enterprises by Foreign Investors	国务院办公厅关于建立外国投资者并购境内企业安全审查制度的通知	03/02/2011	04/03/2011		State Council (*GuoBanFa 2011/6*)
2011 Security Review Provisions	Provisions on the Implementation of the Security Review System for Mergers and Acquisitions of Domestic Enterprises by Foreign Investors	商务部实施外国投资者并购境内企业安全审查制度的规定	25/08/2011	01/09/2011		MOFCOM (*2011/53*)
2012 Enterprise Names Registration Provisions	Administrative Provisions on the Registration of Enterprise Names	企业名称登记管理规定（2012年修订）	09/11/2012	01/01/2013		State Council (*2012/628*)
2012 FIE Equity Contribution Provisions	Interim Provisions on Equity Contributions Involving Foreign-Funded Enterprises	商务部关于涉及外商投资企业股权出资的暂行规定	21/9/2012	22/10/2012	28/10/2015	MOFCOM (*2015/2*)

Short-Form English Name	*Full English Name*	*Full Chinese Name*	*Issued (d/m/y)*	*Effective (d/m/y)*	*Last Amended*	*Issued By*
2012 Forex FDI Circular	Notice on Further Improving and Adjusting Foreign Exchange Administration Policies for Direct Investment	国家外汇管理局关于进一步改进和调整直接投资外汇管理政策的通知	19/11/2012	17/12/2012	04/05/2015	SAFE (*HuiFa 2015/20*)
2013 Foreign Debt Administrative Measures	Administrative Measures for Registration of Foreign Debts	国家外汇管理局关于发布《外债登记管理办法》的通知	28/04/2013	13/05/2013	09/06/2016	SAFE (*HuiFa 2016/16*)
2013 Foreign Debt Registration Guidelines	Operation Guidelines for Administration of Registration of Foreign Debts	外债登记管理操作指引	28/04/2013	13/05/2013	04/05/2015	SAFE (*HuiFa 2015/20*)
2013 Forex FDI Provisions	Provisions on the Foreign Exchange Administration of Inbound Direct Investment by Foreign Investors	外国投资者境内直接投资外汇管理规定	10/05/2013	13/05/2013	10/10/2018	SAFE (*HuiFa 2013/21*)
2013 RMB Direct Investment Announcement	Announcement on Issues Concerning Cross-Border RMB Direct Investment	关于跨境人民币直接投资有关问题的公告	03/12/2013	01/01/2014		MOFCOM (*2013/87*)
2013 RQFII Implementation Provisions	The Provisions on the Implementation of the Pilot Measures on Securities Investment in Mainland China by Renminbi Qualified Foreign Institutional Investors	关于实施《人民币合格境外机构投资者境内证券投资试点办法》的规定	01/03/2013	01/03/2013		CSRC (*2013/14*)

Short-Form English Name	*Full English Name*	*Full Chinese Name*	*Issued (d/m/y)*	*Effective (d/m/y)*	*Last Amended*	*Issued By*
2013 Shanghai FTZ WFOE Medical Institutions Tentative Measures	Tentative Measures for the Administration of Wholly Foreign-Owned Medical Institutions in the Shanghai Free Trade Zone	上海市人民政府办公厅关于转发市卫生计生委等三部门制订的《中国（上海）自由贸易试验区外商独资医疗机构管理暂行办法》的通知	13/11/2013	13/11/2013		Shanghai Municipality Government (*HuFuBanFa 2013/63*)
2014 Cash Pooling Circular	Circular Regarding Matters Relating to the Expansion of Centralized Cross-Border CNY Operations by Multinational Corporations	中国人民银行关于跨国企业集团开展跨境人民币资金集中运营业务有关事宜的通知	01/11/2014	01/11/2014		PBOC (*YinFa 2014/324*)
2014 Company Registration Regulations	Administrative Regulations of the People's Republic of China on Company Registration	中华人民共和国公司登记管理条例（2014年修订）	19/02/2014	01/03/2014	06/02/2016	State Council (*2016/666*)
2014 Cross-border Guarantee Provisions	Provisions on the Foreign Exchange Administration of Cross-Border Guarantees	国家外汇管理局关于发布《跨境担保外汇管理规定》的通知	12/05/2014	01/06/2014		SAFE (*HuiFa 2014/29*)
2014 Draft NDRC Approval Rules Decision	Decision on Amending Certain Provisions of the Administrative Measures on the Approval and Recording of Overseas Investment Projects	国家发展改革委关于修改《境外投资项目核准和备案管理办法》和《外商投资项目核准和备案管理办法》有关条款的决定	27/12/2014	27/12/2014		NDRC (*2014/20*)

Short-Form English Name	*Full English Name*	*Full Chinese Name*	*Issued (d/m/y)*	*Effective (d/m/y)*	*Last Amended*	*Issued By*
2014 FICLS Conversion Letter	Letter on Issues concerning the Transformation of Chinese-Foreign Equity Joint Ventures and Other Types of Enterprises into Foreign-Funded Joint Stock Companies	商务部办公厅关于中外合资经营等类型企业转变为外商投资股份有限公司有关问题的函	24/06/2014	24/06/2014		MOFCOM (*ShangBanZiHan 2014/516*)
2014 FIE Administration Improving Notice	Notice on Improving the Administration of Foreign Investment Review	商务部关于改进外资审核管理工作的通知	17/06/2014	17/06/2014		MOFCOM
2014 Forex Settlement by Banks Measures	Administrative Measures for the Foreign Exchange Settlement and Sale Business of Banks	银行办理结售汇业务管理办法	22/06/2014	01/08/2014		PBC (*2014/2*)
2014 NDRC Approval Rules	Administrative Measures for Approval and Record-filing of Foreign Investment Projects	外商投资项目核准和备案管理办法	17/05/2014	17/06/2014	27/12/2014	NDRC (*2014/12*)
2014 NDRC Approval Rules Amendment	Decision on Amending Certain Provisions of the Administrative Measures on the Approval and Recording of Overseas Investment Projects	国家发展改革委关于修改《境外投资项目核准和备案管理办法》和《外商投资项目核准和备案管理办法》有关条款的决定	27/12/2014	27/12/2014		NDRC (*2014/20*)
2014 Outbound Investment Rules	Outbound Investment Administrative Rules	境外投资管理办法	06/09/2014	06/10/2014		MOFCOM (*2014/3*)
2014 Registered Capital Decision	Decision on Repealing and Amending Some Administrative Regulations	国务院关于废止和修改部分行政法规的决定	19/02/2014	01/03/2014		State Council (*2014/648*)

Short-Form English Name	*Full English Name*	*Full Chinese Name*	*Issued (d/m/y)*	*Effective (d/m/y)*	*Last Amended*	*Issued By*
2014 Registered Capital Provisions	Administrative Provisions on the Registration of the Registered Capital of Companies	公司注册资本登记管理规定（2014）	20/02/2014	01/03/2014		SAMR (*2014/64*)
2014 Shanghai FTZ Cash Pooling Notice	Notice on Broadening the Use of Offshore CNY in the Shanghai Free Trade Zone	中国人民银行上海总部关于支持中国（上海）自由贸易试验区扩大人民币跨境使用的通知	20/02/2014	20/02/2014		Shanghai Head Office of PBOC (*YinZongBuFa 2014/22*)
2014 Shanghai FTZ Shipping Announcement	Announcement on the Pilot Implementation of Increased Foreign Investment Ratio in International Shipping and International Ship Management Services in China (Shanghai) Pilot Free Trade Zone	交通运输部关于中国（上海）自由贸易试验区试行扩大国际船舶运输和国际船舶管理业务外商投资比例实施办法的公告	27/01/2014	27/01/2014		Ministry of Transport (*2014/2*)
2014 Shanghai FTZ Telecom Notice	Notice on Issuing the Administrative Measures for the Pilot Operation of the Value-Added Telecommunications Business by Foreign Investors in China (Shanghai) Pilot Free Trade Zone	工业和信息化部关于印发《中国(上海)自由贸易试验区外商投资经营增值电信业务试点管理办法》的通知	15/04/2014	15/04/2014		MIIT (*GongXinBuTong 2014/130*)
2014 Shanghai FTZ Telecom Opinions	Opinions on Further Opening Up the Value-Added Telecommunication Services in China (Shanghai) Pilot Free Trade Zone	工业和信息化部、上海市人民政府关于中国(上海)自由贸易试验区进一步对外开放增值电信业务的意见	06/01/2014	06/01/2014		MIIT, Shanghai Municipal People's Government

Short-Form English Name	*Full English Name*	*Full Chinese Name*	*Issued (d/m/y)*	*Effective (d/m/y)*	*Last Amended*	*Issued By*
2014 WFOE Hospitals Notice	Notice of the National Health and Family Planning Commission and the Ministry of Commerce on Carrying out the Pilot Program of Setting up Wholly Foreign-Owned Hospitals	国家卫生和计划生育委员会、商务部关于开展设立外资独资医院试点工作的通知	25/07/2014	25/07/2014		National Health and Family Planning Commission and MOFCOM (*GuoWeiYiHan 2014/244*)
2015 Business Licence First Circular	Circular on Strictly Implementing the Reform of Issuing a Licence before an Operating Permit and Business Registration Matters Subject to Ex-ante Approval	工商总局关于严格落实先照后证改革严格执行工商登记前置审批事项的通知	11/05/2015	11/05/2015	24/06/2016	SAMR (*GongShangQiZhuZi 2016/117*)
2015 Cash Pooling Notice	Notice on Further Facilitating Two-Way Cross-Border CNY Cash Pooling by Multinational Corporations	中国人民银行关于进一步便利跨国企业集团开展跨境双向人民币资金池业务的通知	05/09/2015	05/09/2015		PBOC (*YinFa 2015/279*)
2015 FIE Registered Capital Decision	Decision on Revising Certain Regulations and Regulated Documents	商务部关于修改部分规章和规范性文件的决定	28/10/2015	28/10/2015		MOFCOM (*2015/2*)
2015 FIVCC Regulations	Regulations on the Administration of Foreign-Invested Venture Capital Companies (Revised in 2015)	外商投资创业投资企业管理规定（2015年修订）	28/10/2015	28/10/2015		Ministry of Commerce (2015/2)
2015 Forex FDI Circular	Circular on Further Simplifying and Improving Policies for Foreign Exchange Administration for Direct Investment	国家外汇管理局关于进一步简化和改进直接投资外汇管理政策的通知	13/02/2015	01/06/2015		SAFE (*HuiFa 2015/13*)

Short-Form English Name	*Full English Name*	*Full Chinese Name*	*Issued (d/m/y)*	*Effective (d/m/y)*	*Last Amended*	*Issued By*
2015 Forex Reform Circular	Circular Concerning Reform of the Administrative Approaches to Settlement of Foreign Exchange Capital of Foreign-invested Enterprises	国家外汇管理局关于改革外商投资企业外汇资本金结汇管理方式的通知	30/03/2015	01/06/2015		SAFE (*HuiFa 2015/19*)
2015 Forex Settlement by Banks Measures Implement Rules	Circular of the State Administration of Foreign Exchange on Issuing the Implementing Rules for the Administrative Measures for the Foreign Exchange Settlement and Sale Business of Banks	国家外汇管理局关于印发《银行办理结售汇业务管理办法实施细则》的通知	25/12/2014	01/01/2015		SAFE (*HuiFa 2014/53*)
2015 FTZ Security Review Circular	Circular on Issuing the Tentative Measures for the National Security Review of Foreign Investment in Pilot Free Trade Zones	国务院办公厅关于印发自由贸易试验区外商投资国家安全审查试行办法的通知	08/04/2015	08/05/2015		State Council (*GuoBanFa 2015/24*)
2015 HK and MO Law Firms Administrative Measures	Administrative Measures for the Representative Offices of Law Firms of the Hong Kong Special Administrative Region and Macao Special Administrative Region Based in the Mainland (Revised in 2015) (Only Title Translated)	香港、澳门特别行政区律师事务所驻内地代表机构管理办法（2015年修订）	27/04/2015	01/06/2015		Ministry of Justice (2015/134)

Short-Form English Name	*Full English Name*	*Full Chinese Name*	*Issued (d/m/y)*	*Effective (d/m/y)*	*Last Amended*	*Issued By*
2015 Industry Licences Adjustment	Decision on Issues Concerning Cancelling and Adjusting a Batch of Administrative Examination and Approval Items	国务院关于取消和调整一批行政审批项目等事项的决定	24/02/2015	24/02/2015		State Council (*GuoFa 2015/11*)
2015 NDRC Foreign Debt Circular	Circular on Promoting the Administrative Reform of the Record-Filing and Registration System for the Issuance of Foreign Debts by Enterprises	国家发展改革委关于推进企业发行外债备案登记制管理改革的通知	14/09/2015	14/09/2015		NDRC (*FaGaiWaiZi 2015/2044*)
2015 Registration Reform Opinions	Opinions on Accelerating the Registration Reform of Consolidating Three Certificates into One Certificate	国务院办公厅关于加快推进”三证合一”登记制度改革的意见	23/06/2015	23/06/2015		State Council (*GuoBanFa 2015/50*)
2015 SAT Public Notice No. 7	Announcement of the State Administration of Taxation on Several Issues Relating to Enterprise Income Tax on Transfer of Assets between Non-resident Enterprises	国家税务总局关于非居民企业间接转让财产企业所得税若干问题的公告	03/02/2015	03/02/2015		SAT (2015/07)
2015 Tianjin, Guangdong and Fujian FTZ Circular	Circular on Printing and Issuing of the Overall Plan of the China (Tianjin) Pilot Free Trade Zone (also Guangdong and Fujian)	国务院关于印发中国（天津）自由贸易试验区总体方案的通知（还有广东和福建）	08/04/2015	08/04/2015		State Council (*GuoFa 2015/19*)
2016 Business Licence Reform Notice	Circular on Accelerating the Registration System Reform of Five Certificates into One with a Unified Credit Code	国务院办公厅关于加快推进”五证合一、一照一码”登记制度改革的通知	30/06/2016	30/06/2016		State Council (*GuBanFa 2016/53*)

Short-Form English Name	*Full English Name*	*Full Chinese Name*	*Issued (d/m/y)*	*Effective (d/m/y)*	*Last Amended*	*Issued By*
2016 Capital Account Reform Circular	Circular on Reforming and Regulating Policies on the Control over Foreign Exchange Settlement of Capital Accounts	国家外汇管理局关于改革和规范资本项目结汇管理政策的通知	09/06/2016	09/06/2016		SAFE (*HuiFa 2016/16*)
2016 Draft Outbound Investment Record-filing Measures	Administrative Measures for the Verification and Record-Filing on Outbound Investments Projects	国家发展改革委关于就修订《境外投资项目核准和备案管理办法》向社会公开征求意见的公告	13/04/2016			NDRC
2016 FIE Authorized Registration Administrative Measures	Administrative Measures for the Authorized Registration of Foreign-Invested Enterprises (Revised in 2016)	外商投资企业授权登记管理办法（2016年修订）	29/04/2016	29/04/2016		SAMR(2016/86)
2016 FIE Filing Circular	Circular On Expediting Registration For Foreign-Invested Enterprises after the Implementation of Filing Administration	关于做好外商投资企业实行备案管理后有关登记注册工作的通知	30/09/2016	30/09/2016		SAMR (*GongShangQi ZhuZi 2016/189*)
2016 FIE Filing Decision	Decision on Revising Four Laws Including the Law on Wholly Foreign-Owned Enterprises	全国人民代表大会常务委员会关于修改《中华人民共和国外资企业法》等四部法律的决定	03/09/2016	01/10/2016		Standing Committee NPC (*2016/51*)
2016 FIE Filing Interpretation	Interpretation of the Temporal Method of the Establishment and Alteration Filing Management of Foreign-invested Enterprises	商务部条约法律司负责人就《外商投资企业设立及变更备案管理暂行办法》进行解读	08/10/2016			MOFCOM

Short-Form English Name	*Full English Name*	*Full Chinese Name*	*Issued (d/m/y)*	*Effective (d/m/y)*	*Last Amended*	*Issued By*
2016 FIE Filing Measures	Provisional Measures for Filing Administration of Establishment and Changes of Foreign-Invested Enterprises	外商投资企业设立及变更备案管理暂行办法	08/10/2016	08/10/2016	30/07/2017	MOFCOM (*2017/2*)
2016 FIIC Administrative Regulations	Administrative Regulations of the People's Republic of China on Foreign-Invested Insurance Companies (Revised in 2016)	中华人民共和国外资保险公司管理条例（2016年修订）	06/02/2016	06/02/2016		State Council (*2016/666*)
2016 Mainland Measures	Decision on Temporarily Adjusting the Administrative Approvals and the Special Administrative Measures for Market Access concerning Hong Kong and Macau Service Providers in Mainland China	国务院关于在内地对香港、澳门服务提供者暂时调整有关行政审批和准入特别管理措施的决定	31/05/2016	01/06/2016		State Council (*GuoFa2016/32*)
2016 Negative List Announcement	Announcement of the National Development and Reform Commission and the Ministry of Commerce	中华人民共和国国家发展和改革委员会、中华人民共和国商务部公告2016年第22号	08/10/2016	08/10/2016		NDRC, MOFCOM (*2016/22*)
2016 SOE Trading Measures	Measures for the Supervision and Administration of the Trading of State-Owned Assets in Enterprises	企业国有资产交易监督管理办法	24/06/2016	24/06/2016		SASAC, Ministry of Finance (*2016/32*)
2016 Stock Connect Provisions	Several Provisions on the Interconnection Mechanism for Mainland and Hong Kong Stock Markets	内地与香港股票市场交易互联互通机制若干规定	30/09/2016	30/09/2016		CSRC (*2016/128*)

Short-Form English Name	*Full English Name*	*Full Chinese Name*	*Issued (d/m/y)*	*Effective (d/m/y)*	*Last Amended*	*Issued By*
2017 Foreign Debt Notice	Circular on Matters relating to the Macro-Prudential Management of Full-Covered Cross-Border Financing	中国人民银行关于全口径跨境融资宏观审慎管理有关事宜的通知	12/01/2017	12/01/2017		PBOC (*YinFa 2017/9*)
2017 Legal Services for Foreign Affairs Options	Opinions on Developing the Sector of Legal Services for Foreign Affairs	关于发展涉外法律服务业的意见	01/09/2017	01/09/2017		Ministry of Commerce, Ministry of Justice, Ministry of Foreign Affairs, Legislative Affairs Office of the State Council
2017 MOF Repealed and Revised Decision	Decision of the Ministry of Finance on Abolishing Some Rules and Normative Documents	财政部关于废止部分规章和规范性文件的决定	11/12/2017	11/12/2017		Ministry of Finance (*2017/28*)
2017 NDRC Approval Rules	Circular on Effectively Implementing Foreign Capital-related Work in the Catalog of Investment Projects Subject to Governmental Approval (2016 Version)	国家发展改革委关于做好贯彻落实《政府核准的投资项目目录（2016年本）》有关外资工作的通知	14/01/2017	14/01/2017		NDRC (*FaGaiWaiZiGui 2017/111*)
2017 Notice on Promoting Foreign Investment Growth	Notice of the State Council on Several Measures for Promoting Foreign Investment Growth	国务院关于促进外资增长若干措施的通知	08/08/2017	08/08/2017		State Council (2017/39)

Short-Form English Name	*Full English Name*	*Full Chinese Name*	*Issued (d/m/y)*	*Effective (d/m/y)*	*Last Amended*	*Issued By*
2017 SAFE Notice on Promoting Foreign Exchange Control	Notice of State Administration of Foreign Exchange on Improving the Check of Authenticity and Compliance to further Promote Foreign Exchange Control	国家外汇管理局关于进一步推进外汇管理改革完善真实合规性审核的通知	26/01/2017	26/01/2017		SAFE (HuiFa 2017/03)
2017 Unlicenced Business Measures	Measures for Investigating and Punishing Unlicenced Business Operations	无证无照经营查处办法	06/08/2017	01/10/2017		State Council(2017/684)
2018 ALM of FFB Implementing Measures	Implementing Measures of the China Banking Regulatory Commission for Administrative Licensing Matters relating to Foreign-Funded Banks (Revised in 2018)	中国银监会外资银行行政许可事项实施办法（2018年修订）	13/02/2018	13/02/2018		CBRC(2018/3)
2018 Catalogue of Sensitive Industries	Notice of the National Development and Reform Commission on Issuing the Catalogue of Sensitive Industries for Outbound Investment (Edition 2018)	国家发展改革委关于发布《境外投资敏感行业目录（2018年版）》的通知	31/01/2018	01/03/2018		NDRC (FaGai-WaiZi 2018/251)
2018 CNY Qualified FII on Domestic Secunties Circular	Circular on Issues concerning the Administration of Domestic Securities Investment by CNY Qualified Foreign Institutional Investors	中国人民银行、国家外汇管理局关于人民币合格境外机构投资者境内证券投资管理有关问题的通知	12/06/2018	12/06/2018		PBOC and SAFE (*YinFa 2018/157*)
2018 FISC Administrative Measures	Administrative Measures of Foreign-Invested Securities Companies	外商投资证券公司管理办法	28/04/2018	28/04/2018		CSRC(2018/140)

Short-Form English Name	*Full English Name*	*Full Chinese Name*	*Issued (d/m/y)*	*Effective (d/m/y)*	*Last Amended*	*Issued By*
2018 FTZ Negative List	Special Administrative Measures (Negative List) for Foreign Investment Access in Pilot Free Trade Zones (2018 Edition)	自由贸易试验区外商投资准入特别管理措施（负面清单）	30/06/2018（2018年版）	30/07/2018		NDRC and MOFCOM (2018/19)
2018 Insurance Equity Interest Measures	Administrative Measures for the Equity of Insurance Companies	保险公司股权管理办法	02/03/2018	10/04/2018		CIRC (*2018/5*)
2018 Listed SOE Measures	Measures for the Supervision and Administration of the State-owned Equity of Listed Companies	上市公司国有股权监督管理办法	16/05/2018	01/07/2018		SASAC, Ministry of Finance, and CSRC(2018/36)
2018 Measures on Filing	Provisional Measures on Administration of Filing for Establishment and Change of Foreign Investment Enterprises(2018 Revised)	外商投资企业设立及变更备案管理暂行办法（2018修订）	2018/06/29	2018/06/30		MOFCOM (Order No.6)
2018 MOFCOM Repealed and Revised Decision	Decision of the Ministry of Commerce on Repealing and Revising Some Rules	商务部关于废止和修改部分规章的决定	22/02/2018	22/02/2018		MOFCOM (2018/1)
2018 MOHURD and MOFCOM Repealed and Revised Decision	Decision of the Ministry of Housing and Urban-rural Development and the Ministry of Commerce on Abolishing Department Rules Including the Provisions on the Administration of Foreign-Invested Construction Design Entesssrprises	住房城乡建设部、商务部关于废止《外商投资建设工程设计企业管理规定》等部门规章的决定	31/10/2018	31/10/2018		MOHURD and MOFCOM (*2018/44*)

Short-Form English Name	Full English Name	Full Chinese Name	Issued (d/m/y)	Effective (d/m/y)	Last Amended	Issued By
2018 Notice on Active and Effective Utilization of Foreign Investment	Notice of the State Council on Several Measures for Active and Effective Utilization of Foreign Investment to Promote High-Quality Economic Growth	国务院关于积极有效利用外资推动经济高质量发展若干措施的通知	10/06/2018	10/06/2018		State Council (GuoFa 2018/19)
2018 OIE Measures	Administrative Measures for the Outbound Investment of Enterprises	企业境外投资管理办法	26/12/2017	01/03/2018		NDRC(2017/11)
2018 Outbound Investment Measures	Administrative Measures for the Outbound Investment by Enterprises	企业境外投资管理办法	26/12/2017	01/03/2018		NDRC (Order No.11)
2018 PRF of FATE Examination and Approval Measures	Administrative Measures for the Examination and Approval of the Permanent Representative Offices of Foreign Air Transport Enterprises	外国航空运输企业常驻代表机构审批管理办法	22/05/2018	01/09/2018		Ministry of Transport (2018/9)
2018 SASAC on Clearing-up Announcement	Announcement of the State-owned Assets Supervision and Administration Commission of the State Council on the publication of the results of clearing up the existing rules and normative documents	国务院国资委关于公布规章规范性文件清理结果的公告	29/12/2017	29/12/2017		SCAC(2017/1)

Short-Form English Name	*Full English Name*	*Full Chinese Name*	*Issued (d/m/y)*	*Effective (d/m/y)*	*Last Amended*	*Issued By*
2018 Shanghai FTZ Negative List	Special Administrative Measures (Negative List) for Cross-border Trade in Services in China (Shanghai) Pilot Free Trade Zone (2018)	中国（上海）自由贸易试验区跨境服务贸易特别管理措施（负面清单）（2018年）.	29/09/2018	29/09/2018		Shanghai Municipal Government (*2018/1*)
2019 Catalogue of Industries for Encouraged Foreign Investment	Catalog of Industries for Encouraged Foreign Investment (2019 Edition)	鼓励外商投资产业目录（2019年版）	30/06/2019	30/07/2019		NDRC and MOFCOM (2019/27)
2019 Draft FDI Implementing Regulation	Implementing Regulation for the Foreign Investment Law of the People's Republic of China (Draft for Comments)	中华人民共和国外商投资法实施条例（征求意见稿）	01/11/2019	01/11/2019		MOJ
2019 E-commerce Law	E-commerce Law of the People's Republic of China	中华人民共和国电子商务法	31/08/2018	01/01/2019		National People's Congress
2019 Foreign Investment Negative List	Special Administrative Measures for Access of Foreign Investment (Negative List) (2019 Edition)	外商投资准入特别管理措施（负面清单）（2019年版）	30/06/2019	30/07/2019		NDRC and MOFCOM (2019/25)
2019 Foreign-Invested Registration Opinions	Guiding Opinions on Registration Management of Foreign-Invested Enterprises	关于依法做好外商投资企业登记管理工作的指导意见（征求意见稿）	06/11/2019	06/11/2019		AMR
2019 Improving the Use of Foreign Investment Circular	State Council Circular on Further Improving the Utilization of Foreign Investment	国务院关于进一步做好利用外资工作的意见	30/10/2019	30/10/2019		State Council (2019/23)

Short-Form English Name	*Full English Name*	*Full Chinese Name*	*Issued (d/m/y)*	*Effective (d/m/y)*	*Last Amended*	*Issued By*
2019 NDRC Notice No. 4	Announcement of the National Development and Reform Commission	中华人民共和国国家发展和改革委员会公告	30/04/2019	30/04/2019		NDRC (2019/04)
2019 New Lingang Area FTZ Circular	Circular of the State Council on Issuing the Overall Plan for the New Lingang Area of the China (Shanghai) Pilot Free Trade Zone	国务院关于印发中国（上海）自由贸易试验区临港新片区总体方案的通知	27/07/2019	27/07/2019		State Council(*GuoFa 2019/15*)
2019 Notice on Interbank Bond Market by Overseas Institutional Investors	Notice of the People's Bank of China and the State Administration of Foreign Exchange on Matters Relating to Further Facilitating Investment in Interbank Bond Market by Overseas Institutional Investors	中国人民银行、国家外汇管理局关于进一步便利境外机构投资者投资银行间债券市场有关事项的通知	16/10/2019	15/11/2019		PBOC, SAFE (YinFa 2019/240)
2019 Notice on Participation by Expatriates of Domestic Listed Companies in Equity Incentive Funds	Notice of People's Bank of China and State Administration of Foreign Exchange on promulgation of the Administrative Measures on Participation by Expatriates of Domestic Listed Companies in Equity Incentive Funds	中国人民银行 国家外汇管理局关于印发《境内上市公司外籍员工参与股权激励资金管理办法》的通知	23/01/2019	23/01/2019		PBOC, SAFE (YinFa 2019/25)
2019 Prohibitions on Abusing Administrative Power in Competition	Interim Provisions on Curbing Abuse of Administrative Power to Exclude or Restrict Competition	制止滥用行政权力排除、限制竞争行为暂行规定	26/06/2019	01/09/2019		SAMR (Order No. 12)

Short-Form English Name	*Full English Name*	*Full Chinese Name*	*Issued (d/m/y)*	*Effective (d/m/y)*	*Last Amended*	*Issued By*
2019 Prohibitions on Abusing Market Dominance	Interim Provisions on Prohibition of the Abuse of Market Dominance	禁止滥用市场支配地位行为暂行规定	26/06/2019	01/09/2019		SAMR (Order No. 11)
2019 Prohibitions on Monopoly Agreements	Interim Provisions on Prohibition of Monopoly Agreements	禁止垄断协议暂行规定	26/06/2019	01/09/2019		SAMR (Order No. 10)
2019 Reporting Information Measures	Measures for Reporting Information on Foreign investment information	外商投资信息报告办法（征求意见稿）	08/11/2019	08/11/2019		MOFCOM
2019 SAFE Notice on Centralised Operation of Cross-border Funds	Notice of the State Administration of Foreign Exchange on Promulgation of the Administrative Provisions on Centralised Operation of Cross-Border Funds by Multinational Corporations	国家外汇管理局关于印发《跨国公司跨境资金集中运营管理规定》的通知	15/03/2019	15/03/2019		SAFE (HuiFa 2019/7)
2019 SAFE Notice on Cross-border Trade and Investment	Notice of the State Administration of Foreign Exchange on Further Promoting the Convenience of Cross-Border Trade and Investment	国家外汇管理局关于进一步促进跨境贸易投资便利化的通知	25/10/2019	25/10/2019		SAFE (HuiFa 2019/28)

Short-Form English Name	*Full English Name*	*Full Chinese Name*	*Issued (d/m/y)*	*Effective (d/m/y)*	*Last Amended*	*Issued By*
Adjusted FTZ Regulations, Documents and Rules Decisions	Decision of the State Council on Temporarily Adjusting Certain Provisions of Relevant Administrative Regulations, Documents of the State Council and Departmental Rules Approved by the State Council within Pilot Free Trade Zones	国务院关于在自由贸易试验区暂时调整有关行政法规、国务院文件和经国务院批准的部门规章规定的决定	25/12/2017	25/12/2017		State Council (*GuoFa 2017/57*)
CEPA	Closer Economic Partnership Arrangements	内地与香港关于建立更紧密经贸关系的安排	29/06/2003	29/06/2003	1/1/2019	MOFCOM
Cross-Strait Economic Cooperation Framework Agreement	Cross-Strait Economic Cooperation Framework Agreement	海峡两岸经济合作框架协议	29/06/2010	29/06/2010		Association for Relations across the Taiwan Straits
Domestic Catalogue	Catalogue of Investment Projects Subject to the Approval of Governments (2016 Version)	政府核准的投资项目目录（2016年本）	12/12/2016	12/12/2016		State Council (*GuoFa 2016/72*)
Draft FSI Measures	Circular of the Ministry of Commerce on Seeking Public Comments on the Decision on Revising the Administrative Measures for Strategic Investment by Foreign Investors in Listed Companies (Draft for Comment)	商务部关于《关于修改〈外国投资者对上市公司战略投资管理办法〉的决定（征求意见稿）》公开征求意见的通知	30/07/2018			Ministry of Commerce

Short-Form English Name	*Full English Name*	*Full Chinese Name*	*Issued (d/m/y)*	*Effective (d/m/y)*	*Last Amended*	*Issued By*
Draft Market Access Negative List	**Circular of the National Development and Reform Commission and the Ministry of Commerce on Issuing the Draft Market Access Negative List (for Pilot Implementation)**	国家发展改革委、商务部关于印发市场准入负面清单草案（试点版）的通知	02/03/2016	02/03/2016		NDRC and MOFCOM (*FaGaiJingTi 2016/442*)
FIB Regulations Implementing Rules	Implementing Rules of the Administrative Regulations of the People's Republic of China on Foreign-invested Banks (Revised)	中华人民共和国外资银行管理条例实施细则（修订）	01/07/2015	01/09/2015		CBRC(2015/7)
FTZ Deepening Reform and Innovation Circular	Circular of the State Council on Several Measures to Support the Deepening of Reform and Innovation in Pilot Free Trade Zones	国务院关于支持自由贸易试验区深化改革创新若干措施的通知	07/11/2018	07/11/2018		State Council (*GuoFa 2018/38*)
Hainan FTZ Commercial Registration Regulations	Administrative Regulations of the China(Hainan) Pilot Free Trade Zone on Commercial Registration	中国（海南）自由贸易试验区商事登记管理条例	26/12/2018	01/01/2019		PCOHP Standing Committee (2018/20)
Hainan FTZ Master Plan Circular	Circular of the State Council on Issuing the Master Plan for the China (Hainan) Pilot Free Trade Zone	国务院关于印发中国（海南）自由贸易试验区总体方案的通知	24/09/2018	24/09/2018		State Council (*GuoFa 2018/34*)

Short-Form English Name	*Full English Name*	*Full Chinese Name*	*Issued (d/m/y)*	*Effective (d/m/y)*	*Last Amended*	*Issued By*
Mainland and HK Arbitration Procedure Mutual Aid	Arrangement Concerning Mutual Assistance in Court-ordered Interim Measures in Aid of Arbitral Proceedings by the Courts of the Mainland and the Hong Kong Special Administrative Region	关于内地与香港特别行政区法院就仲裁程序相互协助保全的安排	02/04/2019			Supreme People's Court
Market Access Negative List	**Circular of the National Development and Reform Commission and the Ministry of Commerce on Issuing the Negative List for Market Access (2018 Version)**	国家发展改革委、商务部关于印发《市场准入负面清单（2018年版）》的通知	21/12/2018	21/12/2018		NDRC and MOFCOM (*FaGaiJingTi 2018/1892*)
Shanghai FTZ Deepening the Reform and Opening-up Circular	Circular of the State Council on Issuing the Plan for Deepening the Reform and Opening-up of China (Shanghai) Pilot Free Trade Zone in All Aspects	国务院关于印发全面深化中国（上海）自由贸易试验区改革开放方案的通知	30/03/2017	30/03/2017		State Council (*GuoFa 2017/23*)
Tianjin, Guangdong, Fujian and Shanghai FTZ Promoting Circular	Circular of the State Council on Issuing the Plan for Further Promoting the Reform and Opening up of the China (Tianjin) Pilot Free Trade Zone	国务院关于印发进一步深化中国（天津）自由贸易试验区改革开放方案的通知（还有广东，福建和上海）	04/05/2018	04/05/2018		State Council (*GuoFa 2018/14*)

www.ingramcontent.com/pod-product-compliance
Lightning Source LLC
Chambersburg PA
CBHW071352230926
51846CB00002B/517
9789403521220